Celestria Noel is the youngest daughter of the Earl of Gainsborough. She was educated at home in Rutland by a governess and later at St Mary's, Ascot. After her debutante season she went up to Oxford, where she read English at St Hilda's College. Post graduation, she travelled extensively and worked in publishing and on various magazines, before becoming social editor of *Harpers & Queen* in 1992, taking over the Jennifer's Diary column. As part of the job she attended all the events of the British social season as well as many private parties and weddings on five continents. She lives in Herefordshire with her husband Tim and daughter Catherine. She now works as a freelance writer contributing to a number of magazines and newspapers including the *Daily Telegraph*, *The Times*, *The Mail on Sunday* and *The Independent*. Her regular Seasoned Reveller column in *Country Life* magazine has given readers an amusing and insightful perspective on events from the Chelsea Flower Show to Cowes Week. She is the author of *The Harpers & Queen Book of the Season* (Headline 1994).

Debrett's

GUIDE TO
THE SEASON

Celestria Noel

DEBRETT'S PEERAGE LTD

First published in 2000 by Debrett's Peerage Limited

British Library Cataloguing in Publication Data

ISBN 1 870520 79 3

Printed and bound in Great Britain by
Polestar Wheatons Ltd, Exeter

Debrett's Peerage Limited
Kings Court, 2–16 Goodge Street, London W1T 2QA
www.debretts.co.uk e-mail people@debretts.co.uk

Debrett's Peerage Limited was founded in 1769 when George III was on the throne, and is one of the oldest and most established names in publishing in the UK. Debrett's has traditionally been best known for its **Peerage and Baronetage** produced under licence by Macmillan; the next edition will be published in the year 2003. **Debrett's People of Today**, however, the annual biographical reference source for contemporary Britain first published in 1988, has rapidly become a flagship product for the company. Debrett's is now a modern publisher with a long list of titles including:

- Debrett's Correct Form
- Debrett's New Guide to Etiquette and Modern Manners
- Debrett's Wedding Guide
- Debrett's Guide to Tracing your Family Tree

The Debrett's name is seen as a unique and authoritative guide to all aspects of social custom in the UK.

To Tim and Catherine

Contents

Preface

The social season is a series of events that takes place largely during the summer months. Traditional events such as Royal Ascot, Wimbledon and Henley have been joined by newer ones such as motor sport's Goodwood Festival of Speed. This book aims to list such events and to give something of their history and flavour as well as information on how to obtain tickets. Events such as The Fourth of June (the Eton prize day) and Buckingham Palace Garden Parties, although considered part of the season, are not included, as they are accessible to invited guests only.

Other events you may find missing are either not sufficiently established as annual events or are in abeyance, such as Queen Charlotte's Ball for debutantes, which has not been held recently. There is still a debutante season on a small scale, although 'debs' have not been presented to the Queen since the late 1950s. It is now only a concern of mothers whose daughters have been invited to take part by *Tatler* magazine's Peter Townend, who orchestrates private parties for the 18 year-old girls. The only debutante event listed is the Berkeley Dress Show held in aid of the NSPCC in which 30 or so debutantes model clothes for the children's charity.

The Calendar of Events table in Appendix VII to this book lists dates of certain sporting seasons and a broad cross-section of the sporting, charitable and arts events. The criteria for inclusion is that an event must have a social side as well as simply being, say, a championship, and that it should be accessible to any reader if they apply using the proper channels.

Introduction

The social season looks set to enter the new millennium with renewed vigour, a fact that might surprise the casual observer. No doubt those secure plutocrats of the Edwardian era imagined Royal Ascot going on in much the same way forever, but, given this century's pace of change, it is slightly surprising that people should still be applying for vouchers to the Royal Enclosure and attending in tail coats and top hats. What is more is that they are continuing to attend in droves. Of nearly a quarter of a million people attending Royal Ascot each year, 10,000 are admitted to the enclosure.

The popularity of some events which form the season is immense. There is, for instance, a two-year waiting list for the charity preview night of the Chelsea Flower Show and many other events sell out months ahead.

It is amazing that the season has survived two World Wars which changed social life forever, the decision by the Queen to discontinue the formal presentation of debutantes in the late 1950s, the swinging Sixties, Thatcherism and the advent of New Labour. However, it has not only survived but evolved. It is no longer centred on debutantes, though they still exist nowadays. The new breed have attitude and A-levels rather than a vacant desire for a husband. The modern season focuses on events – Ascot, Wimbledon and Henley being the big three, although there are many more ranging from sporting championships to flower shows. The essential ingredient is that people attend for social reasons as well as being keen on the event itself, though many are also fans of, say, tennis or racing. There will often be an element of dressing up as well as certain rules and traditions. People go to see and be seen and to take part in the event.

Many of the season's main events are well established. The Derby was first run more than 200 years ago and even the Chelsea Flower Show has its roots in the 19th century. However, others are quite new, such as the Goodwood Festival of Speed, a celebration of motor sport, founded by the Earl of March in the 1990s. Many of the arts festivals and outdoor opera events have grown huge and become so fashionable that they are over-subscribed many times over. Some traditional social occasions such as Chester Race Week seemed in the doldrums 20 years ago but now sell out four months ahead of May.

Booking and planning far in advance is the key to getting the season right. There are scarcely any events now, other than those which are private or by invitation only, which are inaccessible to the ordinary person, but you will need to know how to get into various events and which enclosures are the best once in.

One of the reasons why the season has received such a shot in the arm in recent years has been the advent of corporate hospitality. Many companies have discovered how useful it is to be able to take clients to the opera at Glyndebourne or to watch tennis at Queen's Club. Many will only experience the events of the season as corporate guests, or even corporate hosts, and it can be by far the best method of enjoying such events, with all-inclusive deals providing good value and taking away the anxiety of obtaining the badges and membership that may be required. Indeed, event promoters can seem reluctant to offer tickets to individuals while they are anxious to sell corporate hospitality. Too much corporate entertaining may, however, lead to a loss of atmosphere, with guests never leaving their hospitality marquees to actually see what is going on.

People of the Edwardian era would have no doubt been surprised at the modern boom in commercial sponsorship, which now has a prominent role. In addition, certain events have become public-relations led. The Cartier Polo, with its celebrity guests and glitzy atmosphere is very different from the average polo match, and risks becoming one giant photo opportunity, subjugating the sport itself. At the same time, it does show that the season has the pulling power to attract the younger *glitterati* as well as tweedy old buffers and, as such, has its place. In fact, parts of the season are full of glamour, and are a huge magnet for overseas visitors. In essence, the season is one of Britain's unique attractions.

However, it is no fun if you have misunderstood any vital aspects of a particular event, such as which areas your badge allows access to. You may feel uncomfortable or, even worse, be turned away, perhaps with friends and clients in tow. Strict dress codes still exist but with advance reconnaissance any embarrassment can be alleviated. Apart from Royal Ascot and Henley Regatta, where women are not allowed into the Stewards Enclosure with short skirts or trousers, dress codes are mostly common sense with either suits or smart casual dress prevailing. Smart casual is increasingly prevalent at events and can be hard to judge. Basically it means that trousers for women are permissible, whereas jeans and a T-shirt are not. Men are required to wear a jacket but not necessarily a tie. The secret is to be perfectly groomed. If your hair is neat and you have the best possible shoes, bag, earrings, whatever, then a simple blazer or equivalent will take you almost anywhere. Certain designers and stores are particularly good at clothing for seasonal events and I have recommended a selection in Appendix III.

If you are attending many events, it is sensible to prepare for the fray. This means not only organising your Ascot outfit in good time, but also a visit to a health farm in late March or April. Plan any major hair and beauty projects ahead so that you are as thin and brown as possible before having to don summer clothes which are far less forgiving than winter woollies. When I was at *Harpers & Queen* and attending almost all the season's events as well as weddings and private parties all summer long, I would always give up drinking for Lent and also try to get some winter sun in March, after Cheltenham and before the Berkeley Dress Show, to give me a boost.

The modern season does not need to cost a fortune in special clothes. The English are fixated on occasion wear and

3

dressing up, but the truly stylish keep it simple. A plain straw hat can often beat an elaborate confection, especially if the person wearing it has had their hair done and given thought to the appropriate make-up and jewellery. Hats are worn far less at ordinary race meetings than they once were and, with an increasing number of evening weddings, such as that of Prince Edward/Sophie Rhys-Jones, hats are becoming less of a requirement.

You may spend a fortune on the season if you care to arrive everywhere by helicopter and entertain lavishly in private boxes. However, not every event is intrinsically expensive and there are always alternative ways of doing things. A picnic to which three or four couples bring contributions, eaten in the car park, will clearly cost far less and is sometimes considered smarter than eating in an official dining room. While Centre Court tickets for Wimbledon are beyond many of us in price and availability, there are often less expensive enclosures where the view is just as good. There are also many events with discounted tickets for early applicants or those that are quite inexpensive anyway, such as agricultural shows.

This book lists the various events of the season under headings and gives their history and a flavour of what they are like. There is also a calendar of events, which gives contact numbers and some helpful booking information. The idea is that this practical guide will help more people go out and enjoy what is there. So much that goes on is far better in reality than on television, and some sports events, such as polo and horse trials, have not yet been televised satisfactorily.

Unlike the Edwardian season, when only those in Society were welcome, it is open to all, within reason. It is constantly evolving and reinventing itself, which is why people still take part in such huge numbers. It would be a mistake to think that a particular event was too exclusive to try if it sounded of interest. The press is to blame for making certain events, such as Henley, sound far more snooty than they actually are. Of course there is also an alternative season of sorts, consisting of events such as Rolling Stones concerts which, if not strictly annual, are hardy perennials. You do not need to apply for vouchers to attend Glastonbury or the Notting Hill Carnival, but they are fixtures for many, as is the Reading Festival (www.readingfestival.com). The open-air concerts in Hyde Park in aid of the Prince of Wales Trust are highly popular, but such events are not sufficiently 'fixed' to be listed here in detail.

For others, the season is very much a country one. *"Tis my delight on a shiny night in the season of the year"* sings the Lincolnshire poacher in the traditional song and you can be sure he does not mean Glyndebourne. To some extent the sporting season and the social season are intimately connected.

Traditionally, winter was the season when royalty and the upper classes would be on their country estates hunting and shooting. The summer season was more urban. Even now the season in and around London finishes at the end of July, as most people leave for the holidays. What used to be called 'the Little Season' ran from roughly the time of the State Opening of Parliament, when the Sovereign returned to London from Scotland in October or November until the beginning of the Christmas holidays. The shooting season is at its peak during November and December, but for those who live and work in London it is a weekend activity and events such as charity balls are usually held on week nights. Country dwellers are more likely to hunt and shoot on weekdays, so that rural social events such as hunt balls are normally on Saturday nights. During the summer the rural season centres around agricultural shows and events such as the Game Fair and race meetings, where inhabitants of the town and the country often meet.

You might say that there is now a season for all men (and all women of course), and, although it is not really for children, it is regarded by many as a playtime for grown-ups. No one would expect to go to everything, but there is so much to choose from that you are almost certain to find something to suit you.

Horticultural
Shows

The Chelsea Flower Show

The Chelsea Flower Show is held in London during the third week of May and is the first major event of the season. Like so many events which are considered part of the season it makes those who take part in it jump through a series of hoops. It is held outdoors and traditionally calls for summer clothes, although it may be cold and wet. It is mid-week. The centrepiece is a hot and crowded marquee, the loos are basic with long queues for the ladies. The structure of the show divides people into distinct categories. There is a private Royal preview, an expensive, exclusive charity gala evening, two days for members of the Royal Horticultural Society (RHS) and two days for the public. The grandees are invited to tea, with iced coffee and strawberry tarts, in the president's tent. The rest of us will grab a snack and be thankful for a seat near the bandstand. For some people it is an annual pilgrimage, for others it may be a new experience. Some go because they are great gardeners, others because they think it is the place to be. For all it is quintessentially English. You have only to see the keen-faced country ladies in floral frocks jumping nimbly from the Number 22 buses to know that all's right with the world, or at least with SW3.

Like many of the season's major events it has a long history. Both the RHS and the Flower Show itself have their origins in the 18th century, when John Wedgwood, eldest son of the potter Josiah, approached William Forsyth, gardener to George III, with the express intention of forming a horticultural society. His main objective was *"to collect every information respecting the culture and treatment of all plants and trees, culinary as well as ornamental."* Forsyth contacted the naturalist Sir Joseph Banks, who had sailed with Captain

7

Cook in 1768, and had gained his approval. Banksian medals are still awarded to outstanding exhibits.

The first shows took place at Chiswick House but these ceased in 1858. Prince Albert encouraged a move to South Kensington, to the site where the Natural History Museum now stands, an area which had earlier been awash with market gardens. There were, however, problems with the South Kensington venue and the RHS had to move its offices after Prince Albert's death. Enthusiasm had not waned though and in 1888 a show was held under canvas in the Temple Garden on the Embankment. By 1913 the show had outgrown Temple Garden and moved to its present venue in the grounds of the Royal Hospital. Before the First World War 178,000 people attended the show. Recently this figure has started to exceed 250,000. A mid-19th-century copy of *Gardener's Magazine* said of the show: *"The principal part of the English aristocracy are present and mix indiscriminately with the tradesmen, the mechanic and the gardener. This scene may be enjoyed by men, women and children for five or six hours at 3s 6d each"*. Allowing for inflation nothing much has changed.

The site is huge and it is easy to get confused by the layout. Entry can either be made from the river embankment or from the north. The use of public transport is wise, either by tube to Sloane Square, by bus, or on a courtesy bus from Battersea Park, where some car parking is permitted. The RHS provides detailed up-to-date information on access every year and the daily papers cover the event thoroughly with the London *Evening Standard* being particularly useful. Tickets must be booked in advance.

Once inside you will find the Great Marquee in the centre. Within it are stands from many major nurseries and plant producers, such as Hilliers. Visitors marvel at the plants themselves, obtain catalogues and place orders. However, you can only buy plants to take away late on the last day. Other stands are devoted to certain types of plants – roses, delphiniums, pansies. Each year there is a different thematic centrepiece, such as a ship made from flowers or a model of a famous building. It usually manages to combine fantastic technical prowess with unbelievably bad taste. The marquee can become oppressively busy, so much so that a one way system is enforced and you disobey it at your peril.

At the eastern side of the Great Marquee runs the Avenue, on either side of which are complete gardens, often sponsored by corporations with newspapers and magazines keen to have a tie-in with the event. These complete gardens are reserved for innovative and creative designers either on the way up or at the pinnacle of their profession. The show is always a source of inspiration, whether your garden is a window box or a large country one. Some are based on actual existing gardens – French couturier Yves Saint Laurent's Moroccan garden has been replicated there, while others have themes – a woodland garden or a Mediterranean garden. There is usually a scented garden for the blind. All these exhibits compete for coveted RHS medals.

An array of assorted hardware, greenhouses, mowers, gadgets and tools of all kinds is arranged around the perimeter tracks. It is one of the best places to see the huge variety of containers that are now available, from traditional terracotta pots to ultra-modern shapes made from experimental materials. Garden furniture is mainly displayed south of the Great Marquee along with fashionable garden statuary, and there are also arts and craft stalls and gifts. The large agro-chemical companies display the latest hi-tech weapons in the battle against aphids and black spot, while disciples of the organic movement preach their gospel on various stands.

Further information from:
RHS 24 hour recorded information line
(Tel: 020 7649 1885 option 4).

Hampton Court and Harrogate

There are of course many other flower shows held throughout the country at different times of the year. Among the major ones which could now be considered part of the season is the Hampton Court Palace Flower Show, which is held in early July and is now one of the largest in the world. The Harrogate Spring Flower Show, held in April completes the Chelsea, Hampton Court trio. Harrogate is a four-day show and is the biggest spring flower show in the UK. It dates back to 1934 and is held at the Great Yorkshire Show ground, though a large part of it is sensibly under cover. It is a major social event in Yorkshire as well as being the premier gardening event of its kind in the north. There is also an Autumn Flower Show at the same venue in September, which is very strong on vegetables.

For more information:
The North of England Horticultural Society,
4a South Park Road, Harrogate, North Yorkshire HG1 5QU
(Tel: 01423 561049).

Other Horticultural Events

During February, March and April the RHS stages a series of specialised spring shows at their halls in Vincent Square, with a major show in mid-April featuring a camellia competition. The shows are a splendid opportunity to see the best plants on offer at every stage of the year with everything from orchids to alpines.

Further details from:
The Shows Department, Royal Horticultural Society,
80 Vincent Square, London SW1P 2PE
(Tel: 020 7834 4333).

A major show not under the aegis of the RHS is the Holker Garden Festival held at Holker Hall in Cumbria in June and there is a vast flower show as part of the Royal Show at Stoneleigh Park in July.

Flat Racing

While a love of horses and racing in particular is not essential for the enjoyment of social life in Britain, it certainly helps as so much of British social life has traditionally revolved around the flat-racing season. The Queen herself has a profound, hands-on knowledge and enthusiasm for both racing and breeding horses. Her own horses have won all of the English Classics except the Derby and like most owner-breeders she still strives to produce a Derby winner. King Edward VII is in fact the only reigning monarch to have owned a Derby winner, 'Minoru' in 1909. The Queen attends many race meetings throughout the year, and always goes to the Derby and Royal Ascot.

The flat racing season commences at Doncaster at the end of March and the first big race of the new flat season, the Lincoln Handicap, is run there on the first Saturday of that meeting.

Dress for flat racing is smart, at least in the members' area. Men should wear a suit and tie, and women a dress and jacket or a suit. Tailored clothes work better than anything too floaty or flimsy. Hats are no longer obligatory, except at Ascot and the Derby, but many women choose to wear one anyway. Huge confections are best kept for Ladies Day and you must always remember to try not to frighten the horses.

Newmarket

Newmarket is the venue for the first Classics of the season, the 1000 and 2000 Guineas. These races are for three-year-old fillies and colts respectively. The Guineas meeting is held over the first weekend in May but keen race-goers will have already taken in the Craven Meeting on the same course in April. The Craven is where many of the horses which will go on to run in the Classics make their seasonal debut.

The pre-parade ring at Newmarket is where all the experts are to be found, studying the horses as they are led round under the anxious eyes of owners and trainers. The horses are then saddled up and taken to the paddock, where more inspections take place before the jockey mounts. Newmarket has two courses: the Guineas is run on the Rowley Mile course, which was named after Charles II who was also known as Old Rowley, after one of his horses. Conversely, Newmarket's July course is used for the very popular mid-week July meeting, and for the rest of the summer, when there is a well-supported programme of evening meetings, some with concerts or other entertainment following the racing. The Rowley Mile is used again for the major autumn races such as the Cambridgeshire and the Champion Stakes. Advance booking is strongly advised for the Guineas meeting and the office opens in January. Otherwise, a daily member's badge can be purchased at the entrance. Annual membership is worth considering if you are planning to attend regularly. Sit-down lunch needs to be booked ahead, otherwise it is a matter of grabbing what you can from one of the bars.

For details contact:
Newmarket Racecourse, Westfield House,
The Links, Newmarket, Suffolk CB8 0TG
(Tel: 01638 663482).

Chester

The big meeting at Chester is held during the first week of May following the weekend Guineas meeting, and is very much part of the season, especially for those who live in the North West. The racecourse itself, called the Roodee, is situated between the ancient city walls and the River Dee and is the oldest in England. It is a natural amphitheatre and was used as such by the Romans.

Chester is a wonderful old town, well worth a visit for its architecture alone, and has an excellent shopping area five minutes walk from the racecourse. Like Newmarket, the racecourse is more a part of the town than is usually the case and this helps give the race meeting its unique atmosphere.

The May meeting lasts for three days – Tuesday, Wednesday and Thursday. If one is coming from London, the train is often better than the motorway in providing transport solutions. The station is within walking distance of the course. Helicopters can land on the course with prior permission. The County Stand is the smartest part of the racecourse but it sells out very early indeed. Pre-booking is essential and the racecourse office is open from the beginning of January. Book within the first two weeks of January for the Thursday, the most popular day, and book any restaurant and car parking requirements well ahead of time. Some excellent inclusive packages are available even until a short time before the meeting. They comprise a four-course lunch, with all drinks and coffee, afternoon tea, a County Stand badge and a reserved car park space. Annual members may re-apply each year and have their own area within the Leverhulme Stand. Annual members benefit from numerous reciprocal arrangements with other courses and other sporting events as well as 11 days of racing at Chester itself.

The feature races at the May meeting are the Dee Stakes (for three-year-olds); the Ormonde Stakes and the Cheshire Oaks (for three-year-old fillies). In addition to these they also run the Chester Vase, an established Derby trial and the Chester Cup, a 'staying' or long-distance race, for older horses.

Details:
The Racecourse, Chester CH1 2LY
(Tel: 01244 323170).

York

The following week sees the big spring meeting at York. The feature race is the Dante Stakes, which is often won by a future Derby winner. The equivalent race for fillies is the Musidora Stakes. The meeting attracts both society types, who tend to dress up, and keen race-goers.

It was always said that the form of the new season does not settle down until York, and that many punters do not start to bet seriously until after the May meeting. There is racing here throughout the flat-racing season but the second major meeting, and very much part of the season, is in mid-August. This is a hugely popular and highly fashionable event, with many people opting for picnics. Traditionally, house parties are given in neighbouring country houses for both of the big meetings but there are many excellent hotels in and around York. The August meeting is often called the 'Ascot of the North' and many people prefer it to the real thing. It is a three-day meeting, Tuesday, Wednesday and Thursday. Feature races include the Gimcrack Stakes, the Ebor, and the Yorkshire Oaks. The racecourse, called the Knavesmire, is just outside the city and is easily reached by road or rail from London.

There is a waiting list for membership of the County Stand but daily membership badges are available on the day, though early booking is important for the various restaurants as seating is quite limited. Much of the smartest entertainment takes place in private boxes, and racing luminaries can be seen examining the runners in the paddock area.

Details:
York Racecourse, York YO2 1EX
(Tel: 01904 620911).

Epsom Derby

The Derby is run in early June and is the greatest of the so-called Classics. It is a contest for three-year-old colts and fillies run over a mile and a half, and is seen as the Blue Riband of the turf. It has been moved from its traditional date, the first Wednesday in June to the following Saturday, with the Oaks, the equivalent race for fillies only, run the day before.

Within the Queen's Stand, a big, modern multi-storey building, the dress code is similar to that of Royal Ascot, that is morning suits and top hats for men and smart day dress with hats for women. It is worth remembering that it can be quite cold. In 1867 it snowed on Derby Day. Outside the restricted area the dress code is jacket and tie for men and skirts or dresses for women though, over on the downs, you will find gypsies and pearly kings with their alternative style of dress. There is still a funfair and you will see people arriving in open-topped buses. But the great days of the Derby, when it was essentially a day out for Londoners and even the Stock Exchange would close, are at an end.

In the days before television, crowds of a quarter of a million were customary. In 1847 Lord George Bentinck even moved that Parliament should be adjourned on Derby Day and so it was for many years. By the 1990s it was thought that more people would be able to watch the race if it was run on a Saturday. However, as a consequence of this change to its timetable many have felt that it has lost some of its special holiday feeling as it now has to compete with other popular Saturday sporting fixtures and the calls on their time that busy people have at the weekend.

The Queen and other members of the Royal Family still attend and watch the racing from the Royal Box. There is a good view from the lawn in front of the Queen's Stand, where the winner's enclosure is situated. The paddock has been moved so that it is just behind the grandstand, making everything more convenient. There is a ground floor bar serving sandwiches that is usually not too crowded. However, the first floor dining room becomes very busy while the upper floors are restricted to guests of the sponsors, Jockey Club members and their guests.

The Derby has an illustrious history. It was first run in 1780. Racing grew up in Epsom as a distraction for those who visited the area to take the waters, from which the famous Epsom salts derive their name. The 12th Earl of Derby had a house nearby called The Oaks and when his uncle by marriage, General Johnny Burgoyne, decided to run a race for three-year-old fillies he named it after the house. The night before the race Lord Derby gave a dinner. Guests included Charles James Fox, the playwright Sheridan and Sir Charles Bunbury, a key figure in the racing world of the time. He suggested a similar race for three-year-old colts and fillies and the story goes that they tossed a coin to name the race and Lord Derby won. Thus the Blue Riband of the turf narrowly escaped being called the Bunbury. As it happened, Sir Charles Bunbury had the pleasure of winning the first-ever Derby with 'Diomed', one of the greatest ever thoroughbreds. Good form was preserved with Lord Derby's 'Bridget' winning the first Oaks. The first four Derbys were run over one mile with the distance being increased to a mile and a half in 1784.

Membership and entry requirements need to be checked carefully with Epsom racecourse and you must book early. A two-day badge can be bought for both the Oaks and the Derby (£90 in 1999) which allows access to the Queen's Stand. For £130 you can become an annual member which will allow you to attend all the other meetings at the course throughout the year. If distances permit, this makes it better value for money especially if you are likely to attend the August Bank Holiday meeting which features the Moët et Chandon Silver Magnum, known as the amateur riders' Derby. Tickets for the less expensive enclosures sell out quickly and should also be booked ahead.

Details:
Epsom Racecourse, Epsom Downs, Epsom, Surrey KT18 5LQ
(Tel: 01372 464348).

Royal Ascot

Royal Ascot is a four-day event held in mid-June on a Tuesday, Wednesday, Thursday and Friday. For many it is what springs to mind when they talk of the season, but apart from the social aspect it is a world-class sporting event. It is also still truly royal with the Queen and different members of the Royal Family attending every day and it is amongst the finest locations for Royal watching. The actual course is the property of the Queen, and its chief administrator is Her Majesty's Representative. Currently, it is to the Marquess of Hartington that you must apply for vouchers for admission to the Royal Enclosure. (Full details and the form of words required is given within Appendix II at the rear of this book.)

The Queen gives a house party for the week at Windsor Castle. Before racing starts every afternoon the Royal party drive across Windsor Park and onto the course through the Golden Gates, and along the straight to the stands. They are seated in open-topped carriages drawn by teams of Windsor Greys, and wave to the enthusiastic cheering crowds. Men traditionally remove their hats. The Royal party watches the racing from the Royal Box, which is in the centre of the main grandstand. However, before the major race on each day they walk down to the paddock and stand amongst the owners and trainers to see the runners being paraded there before the runners are mounted and canter down to the start. Before certain other key races the Queen can also be seen walking briskly and unceremoniously through the crowds beside the paddock, making her way to inspect the horses in the pre-parade ring, next to the entrance to Number One car park. It can be slightly unnerving if you are walking along in a daze, heading for the Pimms bar, and realise who you are next to.

Ascot has a long Royal history; Queen Anne inaugurated racing there in 1711, some 70 years before the Derby was first run but a generation after her uncle Charles II had begun racing at Newmarket. Like Queen Elizabeth II, she drove over from Windsor to an area then called Ascot Common. The value of that first race was 50 guineas, a fair sum then. Anne's successor George I, was not fond of racing and Ascot's fortunes waned until the Duke of Cumberland became ranger of Windsor Forest and put himself in charge of Ascot. The Duke of Cumberland was also the breeder of 'Eclipse', one of the greatest racehorses of all time. He was the first member of the Royal Family to be elected to the Jockey Club, which was founded in 1750, which until recently was still the controlling body of the sport. Ascot grew in popularity during the reign of George III, who saw his son the then Prince of Wales's horse 'Baronet' win the Oatlands Stakes. The first grandstands were built during this period.

The Royal Enclosure was initially an area into which King George IV would invite his friends when he ran into them elsewhere on the course. One can readily imagine the

Regency bucks and belles enjoying Ascot, but, somewhat more surprisingly, Queen Victoria loved it when she was younger. Indeed, so enthusiastically did she watch one finish that she leaned too far forwards and broke a window, which had been shut to keep the rain out. Her son Edward VII, was well known for his love of racing which is commemorated in the King Edward VII Stakes, known colloquially as the Ascot Derby. It is worth noting that the races at Royal Ascot have all kept their traditional names, with, so far, no sponsors' prefix, although Ascot does now go in for merchandising, selling a small range of own-brand products. Edward VII's horse 'Persimmon', son of 'St Simon', won the Derby in 1896 and the Ascot Gold Cup in 1897. No horse since has achieved this double.

The Royal Enclosure is, of course, the grandest place to be for Royal Ascot, but if it is not for you, there are other areas with good facilities and a less restrictive dress code. However, it is perhaps a shame not to make an effort for Ascot, wherever you are watching from. Many gentlemen's clubs such as White's and the Turf Club have marquees for members and their guests or you may be lucky enough to be invited to a private box. All tickets should be booked as far in advance as possible, as numbers are restricted. Car parking labels are available in advance from the race-course. Unofficial car parking is also offered by locals in their gardens; however, it is unwise to rely on this as people return to the same spot year after year and get there early to picnic. Individuals hold on to numbered spaces in the Number One car park over the years, even generations, as it is the place for the smartest picnics. However, there are other picnic spots. I personally would avoid the car park in the middle of the course, Number Seven, which is officially designated for the Royal Enclosure, as it can take ages to leave as you have to cross the course to get out. If you do not want to drive there are good train links or you could try booking a chauffeur driven car, mindful of the police, who are especially vigilant of 'drink drivers' leaving racecourses.

When you apply for either your vouchers or other tickets, Ascot will send you its guide to the car parks and the various routes to the course and it is worth studying these to avoid the worst jams. The M4 exit driving through Windsor Park is best avoided. It is advisable to use either the southerly approach via the M3 or go farther down the M4 and arrive from the west. The best way to miss the traffic is to forget lunch and the Royal procession and arrive just in time for the first race at 2.30p.m. However, for most people who want both lunch and pageantry, getting there early is necessary, even though it can make for a long day.

Thursday is traditionally Ladies Day and is the day to produce your best outfit. However, the opening day, Tuesday, sometimes attracts the biggest crowds as the quality of racing is unbeatable. Wednesday is the biggest day for betting with competitive handicaps. Friday is marginally less busy. In recent years numbers in to the Royal Enclosure have been restricted so it may be the only day available to first timers. Partly as a consequence of this, the Friday has become the most popular day for the young.

Generally, the dress code is strictly enforced. Men without hats or improperly dressed women will not be allowed through the gate. Oddly enough, trouser suits are technically allowed but it is best to opt for a suit or dress. Do not be afraid to make a fashion statement, especially with your hat, but bear in mind that cocktail dresses are inadvisable. Remember that too much bare flesh is more likely to cause goose pimples rather than gasps of admiration, English summers being what they are. Pastel and bright colours look good, as do neutrals like cream and even fawn, while some people favour black and white on opening day, à la Cecil Beaton in *My Fair Lady*. Incidentally, in the film, the horses go the wrong way! Linen is difficult, as it does tend to crease and is not at its best after a long drive and a picnic. Lightweight wool or silk work best. In my experience, if you want to do anything other than sit in a marquee, wear low heels as there is quite a lot of standing and walking. An Ascot outfit can double for smart summer weddings and clever dressers can always recycle clothes and wear them in different combinations. A dress and jacket, rather than a skirt suit, is the most practical outfit for women. If it becomes too hot you can remove the jacket and still have a smart outfit. Tight fitting skirts that ride up when you sit down are to be avoided, after all, you may have lunch on a picnic rug or sit down in the grandstand. Wearing all one colour, including your hat, makes small people look taller and always looks pulled together. The Queen often employs this trick. Do not ruin the line of your jacket with a huge shoulder bag but choose a small, smart bag with a handle. Umbrellas can be a nuisance, but rain does ruin hats, so bring one. You can always leave an umbrella, mackintosh or a light coat in one of the cloak-rooms. Many chic women, who look surprisingly warm in their summer outfits, even when it is bitter, are wearing thermal vests underneath. However, beware of becoming too warm, as it is often stuffy inside bars and marquees. Gloves are no longer necessary but you might like to wear a pair. Parasols look dreadful. Plan your clothes as far ahead as possible and choose the hat first. It is far easier to match a jacket to a hat than vice versa. Invest in a couple of hat pins to keep it secure as you can look silly walking along with one hand holding your hat. If possible think about booking a hair appointment the day before, for even under a hat, hair grooming is important. Tiny hats are best put on by a hairdresser the same morning. Some lucky women can get away with scraping all their hair back into a chignon. Continental beauties seem to manage this effortlessly. Younger women with long straight hair can leave it hanging down their backs or try a pony tail. However, there is a tendency among English women of a certain age to have 'Spaniel ears' of unkempt hair hanging down either side of their faces or to have a fringe of some kind showing under the hat brim. Both are to be avoided. The hat should always be on straight, not on the back of your head. Smart earrings work well with hats and some of the best dressed women you see racing wear both earrings and chokers, but avoid anything too glittery.

Fashions change: one year it will be tiny hats and the next huge cartwheels. Regardless of how much of a fashion victim you are, bear practical considerations in mind. Do not wear a hat with too much veiling if you want to be able to eat or drink. Likewise, a hat with a downturned brim can impair vision. It is important to wear what you are going to feel comfortable in. At all costs, you do not want to take your hat off, as hair looks awful having been under one. Remember you may be in your outfit from mid-morning until six or even seven in the evening, especially if you join other people for a post-racing drink. Outsize hats can make short women look like mushrooms. Invest in a full-length mirror and look at yourself in the whole outfit, bearing in mind that proportion is vital and that, even when fashion dictates grunge or mismatched clothes, this is a style that does not suit Ascot. This does not mean you have to be stuck in a time warp but there is a big difference between being chic and a fashion victim.

Ascot racecourse is huge and it can be rather muddling. The two main entrances to the Royal Enclosure are via either the High Street or the Number One Car Park, which brings you in at the far end of the paddock. It is quite a long walk from there to the main grandstand so you need to allow yourself plenty of time. The two most popular bars are the Mill Reef Bar and the Brigadier Gerard Bar behind the grandstand but they become incredibly crowded. The bars on the upper floors of the stand are marginally less full. Right at the top there are seats that are not reserved and which are available on a first-come-first-served basis. The view of the course from here is outstanding. However, giant screens have now been introduced so that, even if you are not very tall, you can see quite well from the lawn in the front of the stand, which is more fun when the sun is out. The book-makers are to be found at the end of the lawn and there are plenty of Tote outlets. Between the stand and the paddock is the winner's enclosure. Sit down lunches must be booked ahead but, unless you are someone's guest in a marquee or box, a picnic is a far better solution.

The four-day June meeting is the only time Ascot is officially Royal Ascot. The other two big meetings are Diamond Day, the last Saturday in July and the big meeting in late September.

Details:
Grandstand Office, Ascot Racecourse, Ascot, Berkshire SL5 7JN
(Tel: 01344 876876).

Glorious Goodwood

Goodwood House in Sussex is the seat of the Dukes of Richmond, Lennox and Gordon. Racing began there in 1801 when the third Duke and his guests organised an afternoon of private sport. The racecourse still belongs to the family and is run by the Goodwood estate. The Duke's heir, the Earl of March, along with his wife and young family, currently occupies the house. The five days of racing which take place on the course during the last week of July became known as Glorious Goodwood and traditionally signalled the end of the London summer season. After Goodwood the London house would have been closed for the summer. Even today, the meeting has an end-of-term atmosphere and many of the people you see there are having a day or two of racing before going off on the family holiday.

Many people stay locally with friends or family, or in pubs or hotels. There is a traditional week-long house party at Goodwood House itself. Some groups of friends take houses for the week and entertain, while those who cannot take the whole week off, come down for a night or two. Those who manage the whole week are far fewer in number than they once would have been and many people simply come from London for the day. Wednesday and Thursday are generally considered the smartest days with the best racing, including the Sussex Stakes and the Goodwood Cup, but Friday and Saturday are popular too.

Set high on the South Downs, the racecourse has a unique position with the grandstand on the brow of the hill facing north over an undulating course with some sharp bends making the races themselves dramatic. In clear weather, you can see across to the Isle of Wight from the stands. Racing on a hot day is perfect as the exposed position means there is a breeze.

Goodwood is not just breezier but less stuffy in other ways than Derby or Ascot. The Queen and the Royal Family do not attend as a rule. Edward VII described it as "*a garden party with racing tacked on*". People wear summer clothes, the men usually favour light coloured lightweight suits and Panama hats, whilst the women dress in summer frocks or suits, often with a very simple straw hat. The Ascot look is too much for Goodwood, which is altogether more relaxed sartorially. Goodwood sells its own range of Panama hats, ties, and other accessories on the course.

Many people picnic in the triangular car park, Number Three. It is by far the most popular and the most fashionable, equivalent to Ascot's Number One Car Park. However, as with Ascot, people hold on to their slots from year to year and there is a waiting list.

The Richmond Enclosure is the smart place to be but is only for full annual members or their guests. Bear in mind that apart from the five days of Glorious Goodwood there are 13 further days, including a top class August meeting and several very enjoyable evening meetings, one of which is on the Friday of Ascot week. Mind you, if you go to that after four days of Royal Ascot then you really are keen. Full membership also offers extra benefits such as reciprocal arrangements with other courses, and also with Hickstead for show jumping and the Sussex County Cricket Club. Full members may order a guest badge for another adult and one junior badge – children under five are not allowed into the Richmond enclosure. In addition, the annual member can buy up to four daily members' badges for each of the five days of the July meeting. Numbers are limited so organise yourself well in advance. Annual members also need to apply for vouchers for the days they attend. To become an annual member you need to have your application supported by an existing member and approved by the executive committee of the racecourse. In short, it can often be more complicated gaining entry to the Richmond Enclosure than the Royal Enclosure at Ascot.

There are of course other areas of the racecourse with good facilities and there is a thriving corporate sector, encouraged by some well thought out hospitality packages. When you arrive you will see a tented village as well as a range of boxes, which are taken over either by individuals or companies. There is also a Turf Club marquee, again limited to members and their guests. Goodwood actively markets itself and at the same time puts up more barriers than many equivalent events. This arises from the need to make the meeting as profitable as possible and at the same time maintain the exclusivity of the Richmond Enclosure. However, take my word for it, it is worth persevering and once you acquire the Goodwood habit, you will find that a visit to the Sussex Downs is an addictive annual fix.

For full details, contact the
Goodwood Office, Goodwood Racecourse, Goodwood, Chichester,
West Sussex PO18 0PS
(Tel: 01243 755055 or 755000).
For Glorious Goodwood book at least three months ahead.

Equestrian Events

The horse-trials season lasts from March until October. Apart from Badminton, the best-known events are Burghley, which is in September, Gatcombe Park (home of the Princess Royal), in August, and Blenheim in the early autumn. Horse trials are often held in the parks of great historic houses.

For further information contact the
British Horse Trials Association, NAC, Stoneleigh Park,
Kenilworth, Warwickshire CV8 2RN
(Tel: 01203 698856).

Badminton

Badminton is the year's premier equestrian event. The sport of horse trials, or 'eventing' as it is sometimes known, was almost called 'Badminton'. It was the 10th Duke of Beaufort, always known as Master (as he was master of the Beaufort Hunt) who saw the potential of a combined training and equestrian competition, then very much the preserve of the military. The 1948 Olympic Games in London inspired him to stage an event each year in his park.

The three-day event actually runs over four days, the dressage is on the Thursday and Friday, with the cross-country on the Saturday and the show-jumping on Sunday. If you manage to arrive on one of the first two days you will find the site less crowded. There are acres of fabulous trade stands where you can stock up on items of country and horsy kit, as well as buying jewellery, pictures and gifts galore. I know people who more or less do their Christmas shopping at Badminton. It seems, unofficially, to be a dog show as well, with every breed you can imagine being led about and shown off. The car park is also an unofficial motor show for every kind of four-wheel drive vehicle imaginable.

The cross-country day is the most popular with up to 125,000 spectators. It is a sport that has never been satisfactorily televised and is an ideal day out for families. Some hardy souls like to walk the whole course; others find a spot by one fence and camp there. The Lake Fence in front of the house is the most spectacular and the best fun. However, it becomes incredibly crowded and so it can be hard to get a good view. Most people wander about and watch at least part of the event on a big screen, paying visits to the scoreboard to check on the progress of their favourite riders. It is very much an international event and many of the top riders are now from Australia and New Zealand and elsewhere, but there is plenty of home-grown talent.

The Princess Royal, herself a former European champion, almost always attends. The Queen returned in 1999 after a few years of absence. The Royal Family party can be seen mingling informally with the crowds or being whisked past in a fleet of Land Rovers. Dress is casual and if you have not got the right things then you are certainly at the right place to buy them.

Members of the British Horse Society and the Horse Trials Support Group both have special enclosures with marquees and closed-circuit television. However, special enclosure passes are not necessary for once. There are plenty of bars and places for food and the atmosphere is all very relaxed. Tickets are available at the entrance but may be booked ahead; special offers are only available in advance.

Details from the
Badminton Horse Trials Office, Badminton,
Gloucestershire GL9 1DF
(Tel: 01454 218375, www.badminton-horse.co.uk).

The Royal Windsor Horse Show

The Royal Windsor Horse Show emerged in a quiet way in 1943. One afternoon, during the Second World War, there was an afternoon horse and dog show, in aid of Wings of

Victory. The event was so successful that a club was formed to run a horse show the following spring. Princess Elizabeth, as she then was, and her younger sister Princess Margaret, won a prize for the best Single Private Driving Turnout in a 70-year-old pony phaeton which had belonged to Queen Victoria. The dog show fell by the wayside, allegedly after a lurcher stole a chicken leg from George VI's plate, but the horse show went from strength to strength. The Queen took over as patron from George VI in 1952.

The Royal Windsor Horse Show takes place in mid-May in Windsor Home Park, effectively the Queen's own back garden, and she is very much involved. She usually attends every day and presents prizes for many of the competitions. A major international carriage-driving competition runs in tandem with the show itself and there is also a separate dressage competition.

There are the usual classes for hunters, hacks, ponies and heavy horses. Arabians and breeding stock of every kind are also shown. There is, of course, show jumping and there are displays and parades of military bands and police horses. A highlight on the Sunday is the British Driving Society Concours d'Elégance, a parade of horse-drawn vehicles of all ages and sizes, driven by beautifully dressed whips, who usually include the Duke of Edinburgh and the Crown Equerry. They drive round the park for three and a half miles before parading in the main ring in front of the Royal Box. The winner is the most elegant. The rules are strict, fancy dress and period costume are out. The carriage must faithfully resemble a vehicle designed before the 20th century but modern materials may be used in its construction. One or two vehicles, including some from the royal collection, are genuine antiques. They are a fine sight, ranging from little governess carts, drawn by a single small pony, to grand carriages drawn by teams of big horses. There is also a separate coaching marathon, taking spectators back into the world of Dickens and Trollope.

In 1970 the Duke of Edinburgh introduced the International Three-Day Driving Event to the show. It is held in the Home Park and the Great Park. He competed successfully himself, at first driving a team of horses and latterly a

27

team of black Fell ponies, bred by the Queen. There are classes for horse teams, pony teams, pairs and singles.

Competing in carriage driving with a team of horses at the highest level is incredibly expensive, comparable to polo and ocean-going yacht racing, and so, most teams are commercially sponsored. The three days of the competition require different vehicles, different clothes, and different skills. The first day it is dressage where precision and control is being tested, the second is a cross-country course of obstacles, including water, and the third day is held back in the arena, driving through cones against the clock.

Dress for the horse show varies. If you are going to watch the cross-country day of the driving you can be casual and practical but it is far from being a jeans and a T-shirt event. For the show itself people dress smartly, especially on the Sunday. You can apply for membership that will give you access to the Club Enclosure and the VIP car park as well as free admission to the whole show which includes a guest badge. You may also become a weekend member or a junior member if under 25. Day member badges are also available for guests of members. Dress in the Club Enclosure is jacket and tie for men with blazer or tweed/dark suit recommended. Women dress in a skirt or smart trousers.

You do not want to look too citified at an event like the Royal Windsor Horse Show but, contrary to what you might think, the horsy crowd tend to look immaculate and obey traditional dress codes. Unlike Badminton Horse Trials, dogs are not admitted.

Details of driving events, which take place all over the country, often in the parks of historic houses, can be found from the British Horse Driving Trials Association (Tel: 01347 878789). Lowther in Cumbria in August is excellent. The Queen and Prince Philip often attend. Details of the Royal Windsor Horse Show (Tel: 01753 860633, www.royal-windsor-horse-show.co-uk.) You could also try www. horsedrivingtrials.co.uk or the British Driving Society (Tel: 01926 624420, www.carriage-driving.com).

Polo

Polo probably originated in ancient Persia but it became popular in Britain when cavalry officers stationed at Aldershot read reports in *The Field* of a game played by Indian tribesmen. The game's popularity grew during the 1870s and, in 1875, the rules were formalised at Hurlingham. The game is now played in over 100 countries.

The polo season runs from the fourth week of April until mid-September, but somehow always seems to be a game for high summer. It was once seen as an army game but gained a higher profile when the Duke of Edinburgh and later the Prince of Wales took it up. The best-known and smartest polo grounds are Smith's Lawn in Windsor Great Park, home of the Guards Polo Club, Cowdray Park in Sussex, and Cirencester Park in Gloucestershire. However, there are many others such as Knepp Castle in Sussex and the Beaufort Polo Club in Gloucestershire which have a variety of fun tournaments and are user friendly.

The rules are quite complicated and can be hard to follow. Apart from anything else, all the action usually seems to be going on on the other side of the field. Teams of four compete, riding thoroughbred horses confusingly known as ponies, since in the early days the mount had to be a maximum of 14.2 hands high. Even more confusingly, most polo players themselves call them horses. Nowadays there is no height limit but the most suitable height is believed to be about 15.2hh. The teams compete to score goals at either end of a mown grass field of 10 acres (some 300 yards long and 200 yards wide if unboarded, 160 yards wide if boarded). The ball is struck with a mallet that is uniquely held in the right hand only. Two mounted umpires, themselves experienced players, monitor the game, and there is also a referee in the stands. It is a fast-moving, exciting game to watch once you get the hang of it. After each goal the players change ends. It has been described as the nearest anyone will ever get to seeing what a cavalry charge must have been like. The mallet is a bamboo cane with a rubber hand grip and a wrist strap to prevent the player from dropping it. The rider will wear white breeches, knee-length boots with spurs and knee pads for protection. On top, he wears a short-sleeved shirt with his number on it and a safety helmet attached by a chin strap. Players usually wear one glove, on their mallet hand. The ponies wear bandages to protect their legs and usually have fairly severe bridles as their brakes need to be excellent.

In England, polo almost ended during the Second World War when Army officers had other things on their minds. However, the late Viscount Cowdray revived the sport at Cowdray Park, his estate near Midhurst in Sussex, in 1947. Since then the game has grown ever more popular. There are now several first-class women players. Polo is popular at Pony Club level and is played at some schools and universities. For adults though, polo, even at comparatively humble levels is still an expensive game and there are rarely more than a handful of young British professionals who go on to play internationally as adults.

The Prince of Wales's success in the sport coincided with the arrival of major commercial sponsorship. Alfred Dunhill is the long-standing sponsor of the Queen's Cup at Guards and Veuve Clicquot Champagne of the Gold Cup at Cowdray. The finals of these major tournaments, which last about two or three weeks overall, are always held on a Sunday and can be glittering affairs. In addition, Cartier International Day, held at the Guards Polo Club on the last Sunday of July, has become well known for the stars it attracts to its exclusive lunch, some of whom stay to watch the matches! There is usually frenzied press coverage, and The Queen presents the trophy to the winning team.

Cirencester Park in Gloucestershire is less glitzy but is the place to find the Prince of Wales on his now very infrequent polo days, mostly competing in exhibition matches for charity.

In the smart enclosures men may need a jacket and tie, whilst women will wear dresses or trouser suits. Smart casual rather than anything too dressed up is normal. The most vital accessory is dark glasses, worn by all polo fans and hangers-on, while binoculars are a help for the serious spectator. Sun hats can be useful and some people wear baseball caps but smart hats are out. On ordinary days, casual but tidy clothes should be fine. Polo is a happy hunting ground for young lovelies trying to attract the attention of rich and glamorous polo players. A polo matron told off one such, appearing scantily clad at a top match. *"We have come to see the ponies legs, not yours."*

Big matches often have a live commentator, which assists greatly in following the action. However, on smaller days you will have to work it out for yourself. The game consists of periods called chukkas, each of which lasts seven minutes with 30 seconds overtime. There are three chukkas in each half of a match in high-goal polo, five in medium-goal and four in low-goal. At half-time, it is customary for spectators to walk on to the field and help tread in the divots in the turf which have been cut up by the horses, thus making sure the playing surface is as smooth as possible for the second half. This is a good reason for *not* wearing high heels. Players change ponies each chukka but may play the same pony more than once in a match once it has been rested. The ponies are looked after by devoted grooms who hold them at the ready for the players at the side of the field.

At the top level high-goal polo is played by about 15 teams in England during the summer season. They will then move on and play in other countries throughout the year, perhaps wintering in Florida or Dubai and playing in Sotogrande in the South of Spain or Deauville in August. Most have a patron or sponsor, typically the head of a multi-national corporation, who may or may not actually play in his own team. So called 'hired assassins', professional polo players with high handicaps of nine or ten, often from Argentina or other Latin American countries such as Chile or Mexico are much sought after, usually with a young player on a lower handicap making up the numbers.

There is polo at most clubs every Sunday afternoon through-out the summer, and indeed on other days and evenings and you can simply turn up, park and wander about as it is not usually crowded. For the finals of big tournaments things are slightly different. Telephone in advance and check. At the Royal County of Berkshire Club, near Ascot, and several other centres, you can even take lessons. Clubs offer season tickets but it is usually okay to just turn up, but contact the club you are interested in for full details. Membership is not expensive at the smaller clubs. Knepp Castle charged £35 in 1999.

Details:

• *Guards: Smith's Lawn, Windsor Great Park, Egham, Surrey TW20 0HP (Tel: 01784 434212 www.guardspoloclub.com).*

• *Cowdray: Cowdray Park Polo Club, The Estate Office, Cowdray Park, Midhurst, West Sussex GU29 0AQ (Tel: 01730 813257).*

• *Cirencester Park Polo Club: The Polo Office, Cirencester Park, Cirencester, Gloucestershire GL7 1UB (Tel: 01285 653225, www.polonet.co.uk/cirenpolo).*

• *Beaufort: Down Farm, Westonbirt, Tetbury, Gloucestershire GL8 8QW (Tel: 01666 880510). Tuition available.*

• *Knepp Castle: Knepp Castle, West Grinstead, Horsham, West Sussex RH13 8LJ (Tel: 01403 741007). Tuition available.*

• *The Royal County of Berkshire Polo Club: North Street, Winkfield, Windsor, Berkshire SL4 4TH (Tel: 01344 890 060). Tuition available.*

• *Cheshire Polo Office: Park Road, Oulton, Tarporley (Tel: 01829 760650).*

• *Toulston: Toulston Park, Tadcaster, Yorkshire HX4 0BG (Tel: 01422 372 5290).*

Art
& Antiques

The Royal Academy Summer Exhibition

It used to be said that everyone should go to church once a week and to the Royal Academy once a year. The Summer Exhibition traditionally marked the opening of the London season, but this no longer holds true. The Royal Academy now stages major blockbuster exhibitions such as the controversial 'Sensation' or popular 'Monet in the 20th Century'. These shows attract huge numbers, but there are many other smaller shows throughout the year, including those in the Sackler Gallery.

The Summer Exhibition, which opens in June and runs until mid-August, no longer takes pride of place but is still highly popular and attracts over 100,000 visitors. There is usually an opening night party, for which tickets may be bought (from the Special Events Manager on 020 7300 5711) and then several private viewing parties in the evenings for the duration of the exhibition. Some private-view parties are by invitation only but others take the form of charity evenings. These can be a good way of seeing the exhibitions, as many of the guests congregate in the rooms set aside for drinks. This can make for a surprisingly peaceful experience in enjoying the art. Details of charity private views can be found in glossy magazines or from individual charities. The prices are usually reasonable, given the donation element.

The origins of the Royal Academy lie in the 18th century, when 22 artists petitioned King George III to establish an academy and "*An Annual Exhibition, open to all artists of distinguished merit, where they may offer their performances to public inspection and acquire that degree of reputation and encouragement which they shall be deemed to deserve*". The first exhibition took place in 1769. At the time it was rare to have an opportunity to view contemporary art but the exhibition soon became popular, except with those artists whose work was rejected. The first-ever exhibition was held in rented rooms in Pall Mall but for half a century thereafter it took place in Somerset House. The steep stairs there proved too much for many art lovers, including Queen Charlotte, King George III's wife, and Dr Samuel Johnson, the famous lexicographer. Gradually the quantity of pictures outgrew the space. The Academy moved to Trafalgar Square and then in 1869 to its present home, Burlington House, Piccadilly, where the galleries were built over what had been the gardens.

In April the alley beside Burlington House bristles with hopeful artists submitting their work to the annual ritual of selection and hanging. Some of the artists are well known, and may also be members of the Royal Academy, others are unknown. The Prince of Wales has submitted his work under an assumed name and had it accepted. Many other famous artists have had a first showing there. What makes it a fun event is that you can actively make your own choices. Almost all exhibits are for sale and time will tell whether or not you have chosen a winner. There are, however, many celebrated cases where an artist who has gone on to be world-famous has formally had his work turned down by the Academy, notably Monet, ironically enough. Tickets for the biggest exhibitions are available in advance. If you are interested in the Royal Academy consider becoming a 'Friend'. Friends get advance information about what is showing and receive priority bookings. It is not restricted – there are about 80,000 members and it is not particularly expensive.

For further information contact:
The Royal Academy of Arts, Burlington House, Piccadilly,
London W1V 0DS
(Tel: 020 7439 7438, www.royalacademy.org.uk).

Other Art Events

Each autumn the Tate Gallery (020 7887 8000) mounts a different major exhibition which would certainly be a part of the season for many people, though it was not traditionally so. There is of course a multiplicity of art exhibitions, especially in the summer and late autumn when areas such as Cork Street and St James's have evenings when all the private galleries are open.

A newer but ever expanding event is the Contemporary Art Fair held at the Business Design Centre in Islington, in January, simply called Art 1999 or Art 2000, depending on the year. Many of the top galleries exhibit but so do smaller ones and, as at the Summer Exhibition, you can buy the works. Information about times and venues is available in the press or from the various galleries.

The Grosvenor House Art & Antiques Fair

This is held every June at the Grosvenor House Hotel in Park Lane. It is a vast international event and has definitely taken its place as part of the season. It is London's pre-eminent art and antiques fair, attracting those on the social round as well as the top British and international dealers and buyers. There is usually an extremely smart but expensive and exclusive charity gala preview evening, but the whole event lasts for about ten days and is open to the public for most of that time.

Dealers from Paris, New York and latterly Hong Kong now take part, though it will continue to be predominantly a British showcase. All the major London dealers have stands, as do most of the major regional ones. Antique furniture, china, silver, jewellery, carpets, indeed the best of what is on offer, is showcased here and, of course, the British love antiques almost as much as gardening, so it can become very crowded. Anyone visiting the fair can be as sure as is possible of the authenticity of the antiques on show as all exhibits are carefully vetted. It is a perfect opportunity to view the works of art which form a big part of our heritage and is a superb spectacle. However, for all but the richest, what it amounts to is the world's most upmarket window-shopping.

Details:
Tickets and further information are available
(Tel: 020 7399 8100).

Other Antiques Fairs

Throughout the year, there are many other antique fairs large and small. Among the major London ones are the British Antique Dealers Association Fair, held in March at the Duke of York's Headquarters off the King's Road, Chelsea, London SW3 (020 7589 6108). The Fine Art and Antiques Fairs held at Olympia and known colloquially as 'Olympia' are held in February, June and November, and are highly popular. (Tickets: 020 7373 8141 for private functions, lectures and corporate hospitality.) The fairs often include interesting loan exhibitions and are well worth a visit.

Trooping The Colour

The ceremony of Trooping The Colour by the Household Division (the regiments of the Queen's Guard) celebrates the sovereign's official birthday. The event takes place on the second Saturday of June. The Queen wears the uniform of whichever of the regiments of Foot Guards is trooping its colour that year – the Grenadiers, Coldstream Guards, Scots, Irish and Welsh Guards take it in turns. In recent years, the Queen has ridden in a carriage but she used to ride side-saddle for many years on her mare 'Burmese', who always behaved perfectly on the day but was considered something of a 'madam' at home.

The Queen leaves Buckingham Palace at 10.40a.m. and proceeds along The Mall, escorted by the sovereign's escort of the Household Cavalry. The Household Cavalry is the mounted part of the Queen's Guard and consists of two regiments, the Life Guards and the Blues and Royals, irreverently known by other regiments as 'donkey wallopers' but not, on the whole, to their faces.

The Queen arrives at Horse Guards, where the parade ground is situated, at the far end of The Mall and at 11a.m. the national anthem is played and a gun salute is fired in Hyde Park. Her Majesty then inspects the parade, which unfolds in a masterly display of drill. The parade ends with all of the regiments marching past the Queen in a procession of slow and quick marches to familiar tunes such as 'The British Grenadiers'. She departs for the Palace at 12.30p.m. with the Foot Guards marching behind her. She reappears on the balcony of Buckingham Palace, accompanied by other members of the Royal Family, often including the younger children, to watch a fly-past by the Royal Air Force at 1p.m.

It is a great spectacle and although it is always televised, the atmosphere is quite different when you see it live. Military music works far better in the open air.

Trooping The Colour is a practice older than the British Standing Army itself. In the early days, a colour was used as a recognisable rallying point in battle. Each company had its own flag to distinguish it from its fellows. From about 1700, company colours grew into battalion colours. These were paraded down the ranks at the end of a day's march and escorted with due pomp to the night's billet, the seat of battalion headquarters and its assembly point in case of emergency. Every man in the battalion thus became familiar enough with his own colour to pick it out even at the height of a battle and the colour came to represent the spirit of a regiment.

The Household Division carried out a Trooping The Colour Parade as early as 1755 but in 1805 it began to perform the ceremony in honour of the sovereign's birthday. With a short break during the madness of George III, it has continued in much the same form ever since.

Tiers of seats from which spectators may watch surround the parade ground. Tickets are allocated by ballot and are limited to two per person. If you are unsuccessful in the ballot for the ceremony itself you may apply to be included in the ballot for the rehearsals which take place on the two preceding Saturdays. The first rehearsal is known as the Major General's Review and the second as the Colonel's Review. They are identical to the real thing other than that there is a stand-in for the Queen herself.

Beating the Retreat is another popular military spectacle. The massed bands of the Household Division 'Beat the Retreat' on Horse Guards Parade on successive June nights.

Details on all the above:
Tel: 020 7414 2353. Address for the postal ballot for tickets:
Brigade Major, HQ Household Division, London District,
Horse Guards, Whitehall, London SW1A 2AX.

Goodwood Festival of Speed

The vast majority of events that make up the season have long histories. An exception to this is the Goodwood Festival of Speed, started by the Earl of March in 1993 in celebration of 100 years of motor sport. Held in June over three days, Friday, Saturday and Sunday, it is now the biggest event of its kind in the world, described as not just a motor sports event but a happening.

Lord March was inspired in his love of racing cars by his grandfather Freddie, the 9th Duke of Richmond. The 9th Duke competed in motor sports before the Second World War. The Festival of Speed itself centres on a one-mile timed hill climb from a position in front of Goodwood House. The racing cars, which include Formula One cars of the Sixties, Seventies, Eighties and even Nineties are driven by some of the legendary names of motor racing including Stirling Moss, Jack Brabham and Emerson Fittipaldi, or by their enthusiastic owners. There are also motorbike champions such as John Surtees. The paddock, where the cars are displayed before taking part, is the focus for enthusiasts and has become a mecca for collectors. There you have the chance to examine such wonders as the 1978 3.0 Ferrari 312T3 F12 which was driven in Grand Prix by Gilles Villeneuve and now belongs to Pink Floyd musician Nick Mason, an avid collector and racer.

Collectors of racing cars and sports cars from all over the world bring their precious cars not just to be marvelled at but for them to be driven competitively once more. Some date back to before the Second World War but it is the great beasts of the post-War era which are the real stars. The event bears little resemblance to a sedate vintage car rally. It is a unique event attracting both experts and families.

Friday is the day to simply stand in wonder, or perhaps picnic and see the cars arriving from all over the world.

Saturday is practice day when you can see them in action and there is also an air display in the afternoon. Sunday features Formula One teams in action, a fly past by the Red Arrows and the Cartier Style et Luxe, a separate 'concours d'élégance' of beautiful old cars such as Bentleys and Bugattis judged by a panel which includes celebrities and designers. Tickets for the Sunday must be purchased in advance. The event runs from 9a.m.-6p.m. but the gates actually open at 6.30a.m. If you want a good vantage point to see the hill climb you will need to be an early bird.

In addition, there is a specialist car auction and dozens of other attractions. Dress is smart casual but the really cool wear driver's overalls, signifying that they are actually taking part. It is not the place for deer stalker hats often worn by veteran car enthusiasts. It is a much younger event with more *vroom*.

In 1998, Lord March received permission to reopen the motor circuit at Goodwood, which had been closed since 1966. It had been used for testing vehicles in the interim but a three-day meeting now takes place in September, with some of the top drivers reunited with the cars they drove in the 1950s and 1960s. Billed as a chance to forget the modern world and remember the glory days of British racing green, the event is still in its infancy but is already proving a success. It includes aerial displays of planes from the same era. Tickets are available on the day but book in advance for the third day and book separate grandstand seats in addition if you wish to watch in comfort. For £50 you can become an annual club member with discounts on tickets and access to a private members' enclosure and paddock areas. As the Festival of Speed is now so huge, good access is becoming more difficult, thus membership might be a good idea. Members will be informed of other special events during the year and will be given a handbook. Children are admitted free but must be accompanied by an adult.

For full details of the Festival of Speed and other motor sport at Goodwood: Goodwood House, Goodwood Park, Goodwood, Chichester, West Sussex (Tel: 01243 755055 or 755000, www.goodwood.co.uk).

Tennis

Wimbledon

Many of the important events of the season run for three days and others such as Ascot, Goodwood and Cowes, have their weeks, but Wimbledon is unique in having a full fortnight. It is held during the last week of June and the first week of July. The English summer being what it is, at least one week usually enjoys 'freak weather conditions' i.e. rain, which can make it difficult for the organisers to fit in all the matches. However, it is rare for the event to run into the Third Monday.

Wimbledon has its traditional strawberries and cream. Equally traditional are the tears from the lady finalists and comforting kisses from the Duchess of Kent. Wimbledon is very much a part of the season but it is also a world-class sporting event, a true championship which in any other country would be known as the British Open. Wimbledon is special. The courts are all grass, perfectly maintained, the original turf is supposed to have been brought from the seaside. The ball boys and girls wear uniforms. Players too have to obey certain rules – skirts for the ladies, predominantly white for all, bows and curtsies to the Royal Box, though not all players observe this custom.

Tennis is an incredibly popular game among the British upper and middle classes. More play it at some level than almost any other sport and it is seen as an essential social grace for their children. However, a great many of them have turned watching Wimbledon on television into part of their domestic social lives due to the difficulty of obtaining tickets, unless you are lucky enough to be a corporate guest. The sight of the Centre Court with empty seats bought by investment banks, whose guests have failed to show, never fails to enrage, but the organisers have lately been making a big effort to counter this criticism. Things have been made

41

easier for ordinary tennis fans. For instance, the enlarge-
ment of Court Number One over the past few years has
allowed a greater ticket allocation into the main ballot.

However, the ballot allocation is still quite complicated.
Between August and December you may write to the All
England Lawn Tennis Club enclosing a stamped addressed
envelope asking for a ballot form for the following year's
tournament, which must be completed and returned by the
end of January. Only one application for a pair of tickets per
household is permitted.

Wimbledon originally financed itself by selling debentures,
almost an early form of time share, which were bought
mainly by wealthy individuals who were keen on tennis.
These debentures are still in existence and some are still
held by the families of the original owners. The idea is that
individuals or, more usually, companies, may purchase blocks
of seats for the Centre Court for every day of the tournament
for five years. Debenture holders also have the benefit of a
special lounge where lunch and tea are served. The debentures are traded on the London Stock Exchange and change
hands for many thousands of pounds. The money they bring
in goes towards improvements such as new facilities. When
Wimbledon began in 1877, no one could have foreseen the
size of the present-day tournament and if they had, a
different site may well have been chosen.

You may be lucky enough to be invited for a day's tennis
by a member of the All England Lawn Tennis Club. They are
entitled to buy a pair of tickets for every day of the
championships and there is an enclosure where they can
have lunch or tea and entertain guests.

You can of course simply turn up and queue for a ticket at
the turnstiles, which allows you access to the ground and all
the courts except the Centre Court, Court No. 1 and Court
No. 2 which are the show courts. In the first ten days you
are likely to see excellent matches on these courts and,
depending on the weather and how many matches have not
yet been played, this might still be possible in the last four
days. You may also buy a ticket throughout the tournament
from about mid-afternoon onwards from the re-sale kiosk
north of court 18 in St. Mary's Walk. These will cost £5

before 5 p.m. and £3 after 5 p.m. Corporate guests, full of lunch, may well only stay for a couple of hours and thus leave their seats free. Hospitality packages are available through agencies, at a price. Touts are to be seen but they should be shunned.

Dress should be smart casual, smarter if you are attending a corporate lunch or likely to be in a special marquee or enclosure. Some women choose to wear pretty summer dresses and a sun hat but it is not really an event to bother with if you wish to be seen and have no real interest in the sport. In short, there is very little of the garden party or promenade involved, in contrast to say Henley, where so many people seem to go just for a picnic by the river or indeed Ascot where some of the crowd seem to keep their backs firmly towards the horses in an effort to see who is who and who is wearing what. Wimbledon fans are real *aficionados*. Unfortunately, the fact that there has been a revival of fortunes among British players has also made them over-enthusiastic in their support for the players they love and there is now too much cheering and shouting for my taste.

For further information about membership and other details contact: The All England Lawn Tennis and Croquet Club, Church Road, Wimbledon, London SW19 5AE (Tel: 020 8944 1066) or write to PO Box 9, Church Road, Wimbledon, London SW19 5AE with an SAE for an information sheet (Tel: 020 7381 7000 for general information, www.lta.org.uk).

Wimbledon's unofficial warm-up tournaments are held at Queen's Club in West London and at Eastbourne in Sussex.

Eastbourne Ladies Championship

Eastbourne stages the Ladies Championships and is very popular in its own right.

Eastbourne Box Office: (Tel: 01323 411555).

Queen's Club

Queen's Club is the venue for the Stella Artois Grass Court Championships, in which many of the top players take part.

It is a popular event, particularly amongst Londoners who might not make the effort to go to Wimbledon itself, and tickets are hard to come by.

Queen's Club's information line recommends that you join the mailing list by sending your name, address and telephone number to the Stella Artois Mailing List, Glen House, Stag Place, London SW1E 5AG. You should do this a full year in advance. You will then be sent an application form six months before the tournament itself which you will need to return as soon as possible as applications are dealt with on a first come first served basis. If you are unlucky there is a credit card hotline which is open from mid-April. If there are any centre-court tickets left you can buy them through the credit card hotline (020 7413 1414) which also sells ground admission tickets for £10, which will give you access to outside courts. Full members of Queen's Club will receive an application form, to be returned by the December before the tournament to ensure first bite at the cherry.

Details for Queen's Club: There is an information line (Tel: 020 7413 1414) or for corporate hospitality packages (Tel: 020 7386 3424). Hospitality tickets are rare so plan six months ahead for these. For details of how to join the club itself write to Queen's Club, Palliser Road, London W14 9EQ, but be warned there is a long waiting list as there is for all of London's prestigious tennis clubs (www.queensclub.co.uk).

Mulberry Tennis Classic

A relative newcomer is the Mulberry Tennis Classic, held for the first time in 1997. The Hurlingham Club in Fulham, West London, hosts this four-day event in June that often coincides with Ascot Week. It is a pro-celebrity tournament in aid of the NSPCC, which looks set to become an established part of the season. A ball is held as part of the event. Many of those who play at Wimbledon take part, as do well-known veterans.

Mulberry Tickets:
Available through Quintus (Tel: 020 7596 3724) or contact the NSPCC London Events Office (Tel: 020 7596 3724).

Henley
Royal Regatta

Henley is the third great set-piece event of the summer season after Ascot and Wimbledon. While Ascot attracts top-class racehorses and Wimbledon world-class tennis players, less is known by the general public about rowing and many spectators leave Henley none the wiser about the sport. It is a shame as the rowing is of a high standard and the regatta attracts 400 to 500 entries from all over the world.

Henley Royal Regatta, to give it its correct name, takes place over five days in early July, sometimes coinciding with the end of Wimbledon. It was first held in 1839 and Prince Albert was its first Royal patron. Since this time, the reigning monarch has always graciously consented to be patron but it is not a regular event for any of the current Royal Family.

Henley has its own unique aspects. It predates both the establishment of the Amateur Rowing Association (the sport's ruling body in England) and the International Rowing Federation. Henley, therefore, has its own rules and is not subject to their jurisdiction, though it is officially recognised by both bodies. Modern rowing competitions usually start with the boats abreast in a number of lanes. Henley is different, as only the two finalists compete in each race, the others having been knocked out in heats prior to the final. Some of these races will have taken place before the official first day. The chosen format has its strengths and weaknesses. It makes individual races easier to watch, but means that in a whole day's programme the races are started at five-minute intervals. This makes for a busy programme with plenty of finishes for spectators to watch but you need to pay attention to your programme if you are to keep abreast of the results. The course is one mile 550 yards long, which is slightly farther than the 2000 metres, which has become a standard at most rowing events.

There are 16 events in total, five classes for eights; five classes for fours; two for quadruple sculls; races for coxless pairs and double sculls. In addition, there are races for single sculls, including, since 1993, one for women. There are some magnificent trophies including the old established Grand Challenge Cup for eights.

Since 1884, Henley has been organised by a self-elected body of stewards, at present numbering about 50, most of whom were competitive rowers or scullers themselves. These include many who rowed for Oxford or Cambridge in the Boat Race and some who rowed for England in the Olympics. Rowing is a sport that Great Britain was traditionally quite good at and for which it still wins medals.

Henley's stewards are predominantly male and public school, many live in the Thames Valley and they take a huge and justifiable pride in Henley, where there is still no commercial sponsorship or external subsidy. It costs more than £1m to stage but 70% of that is derived from subscriptions paid by members of the Stewards Enclosure and their purchases of badges for guests.

The stewards are the custodians of the stretch of river known as Henley Reach. In 1987, they bought Temple Island, restoring the temple by Wyatt, built in 1771. They are responsible for clearing away all signs of the regatta, so that, between September and March, when the setting up begins again, there is nothing there to disturb the tranquillity of the river and its surroundings.

Henley has an atmosphere all of its own. On one level, the event is one of the most accessible of the season. The towpath and the Regatta Enclosure are both open to the public. The Regatta Enclosure, next to the Stewards Enclosure is quite inexpensive. Many have merry picnics in the car park and it attracts many twenty-somethings, singles and young married couples. In big groups of 20 or 30 they go along very much for a fun day and cheerfully admit that, apart from the odd one or two chaps who rowed at school, they know nothing about the sport itself.

However, membership of the Stewards Enclosure is limited to 6000 and there is a long waiting list of people wanting to join. You must be proposed and seconded by existing members. Priority is given to those who have competed in the regatta but even they have to wait several years. There is a one-off membership fee and then an annual subscription. Members can apply to take guests into the enclosure but numbers are limited on the Saturday and Sunday. Effectively it is more of a closed shop than Ascot.

The dress code is famously strict and it seems as though every year the papers show a picture of a girl being turned away for having too short a skirt. This is one of the only aspects of Henley that garners publicity. Photography within the enclosure is strictly controlled which is one reason the papers and magazines do not cover Henley as a social event in the same way that they do with many other parts of the season. This pleases the purists but means that Henley lacks the frothy glamour of some other events.

Women must wear a dress or skirt that covers their knees and are not allowed trousers or divided skirts. Men must wear lounge suits or blazers with flannels and a tie or cravat. Many men wear boating blazers but these should have been honestly acquired, that is, you should have been a member of the rowing team of your school, university or a recognised rowing club. Designer blazers with spurious markings are frowned upon. A plain navy one is fine. In fact the most garish and fake looking usually turn out to be the mark of membership of some very prestigious club. These are immediately recognised and honoured by male cognoscenti and marvelled at by ignorant wives. These same wives never cease to be amazed that men, who normally wince at any hint of colour, lose all sense of style when the thing confers membership of some kind and becomes a uniform.

The most distinctive garb at Henley is a cerise (pink to you and me) cap and tie, belonging to members of Leander. The Leander Club Enclosure is next to the Stewards Enclosure. Full members of Leander need to have been proposed and seconded by existing members and the committee gives precedence to those who have rendered special service

47

to the sport of rowing, so it is very hard to become one. However, there are also associate members, who still need to be elected but for whom the terms are slightly less stringent.

The Phyllis Court Club, which has an enclosure on the north or Buckinghamshire bank of the Thames, is also a private club, but grandstand tickets may be sold to members of the public. There are also hospitality tents which can be booked through Payne & Gunter (Tel: 020 8842 2224).

Whilst Henley has kept itself free of commercial sponsorship, it has still become a popular part of the corporate entertainment calendar. To me it has always been an event where you need to be an insider to see the point. It is very male, very public school and very English. A rich, glamorous foreigner, taken to Henley and told it was a key social event might be charmed but is more likely to be baffled.

For general information about Henley Royal Regatta, contact The Secretary, Henley Royal Regatta, Regatta Headquarters, Henley-on-Thames, Oxfordshire RG9 2LY (Tel: 01491 572153, www.hrr.co.uk).

Arts Festivals

While for many people the word Henley may be synonymous with rowing, for others it has come to mean the Henley Festival of Music and the Arts. This event follows the regatta, held in the second week of July. For a country thought by some to be philistine, Britain is extraordinarily rich in music and arts festivals. Some such events have become very much a part of the social season and are becoming increasingly popular.

Classical music is particularly well served. Apart from Henley there is the Newbury Spring Festival in May; the Bath International Music Festival in May; the Aldeburgh Festival of Music and the Arts in June; the Buxton International Festival at the end of July; the Cheltenham International Festival of Music, and many many more.

The above are all based on classical music. In addition, there are rock festivals, of which the best known is Glastonbury. Glastonbury is now long established, and has become a part of the social season, at least for the young. The young includes many baby boomers who find the mud at Glastonbury as much of a tradition as the strawberries and cream of Wimbledon.

Theatre festivals include Ludlow, which also has music of different kinds, Malvern in August, which now hosts three productions from the trendy Almeida Theatre, based in Islington, London, who use the festival to try out new plays. Add to this the well-established Chichester Festival and many more.

In London, the Open Air Theatre in Regent's Park has a summer Shakespeare season of long standing which runs from late May until early September. These festivals have never had any difficulty selling tickets but their staid image is a thing of the past and they are now fashionable as well as popular.

Glyndebourne

More traditionally associated with the season is opera at Glyndebourne, though do not mention the social season to anyone involved with putting on opera there, as they like to distance themselves from such frivolities. However, like it or not, Glyndebourne is considered a part of the season by many. Its inclusion in this text is ratified by the fact that it is attended by not only opera lovers but also has a strong corporate flavour where bankers and their guests mix with those who wish to impress. It also has the feel of a garden party, as people often picnic in the grounds in the interval. However, there are also several popular restaurants within the complex, which has been greatly extended to include a new opera house.

The dress codes used to be very strictly adhered to, but you see fewer women in full length dresses or skirts now. The management prefers but does not insist on evening dress, although you do need to look elegant.

The Glyndebourne season runs from the end of May until the end of August. There are usually five productions, always sung in the original language. People tend to associate Glyndebourne with Mozart but in fact the works of a wide range of composers, including those who are less well known, may be heard, as well as rarely performed works by some of the major composers.

Other Arts Festivals

Garsington near Oxford is described by some as what Glydebourne used to be. The Ingrams family who own Garsington Manor, once the home of Lady Ottiline Morrell, stage outdoor opera for three weeks from mid-June to early July. The performers are under cover but, depending on seats, the audience is not entirely sheltered. People picnic in the very pretty grounds or eat in the restaurant. In spite of some local opposition on the grounds of noise and traffic disturbance, it is extremely popular and almost impossible to obtain tickets. Ask to have your name put on the waiting list a year in advance.

The most recent recruit to the ranks of country-house opera is Grange Park, near Winchester, in early July (Tel: 020 7246 7567). They usually host two productions, one part of the well-known cannon and one more unusual; they sometimes have a separate concert performance as well. Although it is advisable to book far in advance, with the booking office opening in May, Grange Park has yet to become as difficult as Garsington in terms of availability. The atmosphere is delightful and artistically speaking the standards are extremely high. However, the emphasis is on fun and enjoyment. The evening begins with champagne under the Doric portico while the opera itself takes place in the Orangery. The crumbling plasterwork adds to the ambience and the red plush seats too are worn – they used to be at the Royal Opera House, Covent Garden. There is a 90-minute interval, during which some choose to picnic but others dine in the house in a vast room lit by chandeliers. It is all extraordinarily stylish. Tickets are between £60-£80.

In Holland Park, west London's equivalent to country house opera, the open-air season has gone from strength to strength and obtaining a ticket is becoming as hard as Garsington. The season runs from early June to mid-August. Box office (Tel: 020 7602 7856).

In addition to the above there are various country-house and open-air opera seasons. Freddie Stockdale's Pavilion Opera performs to a piano accompaniment in various venues, usually in aid of charity. Details of such events are usually available through the charities and are listed in such magazines as *Harpers & Queen*, or indeed may be advertised locally. Such performances have a beguiling intimacy. I remember going to see a Pavilion Opera production of Tosca performed at Arundel Castle and loving being able to sit so close to the singers.

Literary festivals are catching up with opera and becoming increasingly fashionable. Hay-on-Wye, a small town in the Welsh Marches, hosts one of the best in late May, usually over the Bank Holiday. Cheltenham takes place in mid-autumn.

Agricultural Shows

The Royal Show

At the opposite end of the spectrum to country-house opera stands the traditional agricultural show. Of these, the Royal Show is the biggest national event of its kind. It often attracts members of the Royal Family and has a smart social side as well as aspects that are more down to earth.

The Royal Show is a vast event attended by up to 200,000 people. It always takes place in early July beginning on the Monday and closing on the Thursday after. Since 1963, it has had a permanent home at the National Agricultural Centre, Stoneleigh Park, Kenilworth, between Coventry and Warwick. The show ground is not far from the M40 motorway and bills itself as Europe's premier exhibition of farming, food and the countryside. It is very much an opportunity for those in the farming industry to both network and shop. All of the latest farm machinery is on display and tens of millions are spent on machinery each year at the show. However, there is plenty for the more casual visitor to see, from livestock to demonstrations of crafts and skills. It is a real must for hobby farmers and those with an interest in country pursuits. In addition, there is a major flower show. There is a country lifestyle area which focuses on country houses and gardens, leisure activities and traditional rural skills. The show serves as a good resource for information on rural issues aimed at all those who live in the country, whether or not they actually farm.

It is run by the Royal Agricultural Society (RASE), whose members and guests have the use of a special pavilion. However, it is not the sort of event where you need an array of special badges or passes and although the RASE welcomes members it would not be worth joining simply for the sake of the Royal Show.

The first show was held at Oxford in 1839. Queen Victoria allowed the society to call itself Royal from 1840. The founders included landowners, agricultural journalists and enthusiasts who were convinced that the application of science would show the way forward for farming. A growing population needed to be fed and greater productivity was essential. Today there are those who think that modern farming has been characterised by over-production and that science has sometimes been misapplied.

However, the RASE states that it has a commitment to 'practise with science' – or encourage the practical application of science – which is enshrined within its crest. The issues however, still remain at the forefront of the agricultural debate. Their house journal, produced annually since 1849, provides a medium for the publication of learned research papers reflecting the contemporary thinking of those leading the developments taking place within agriculture in its widest sense.

If this all sounds too serious then take heart from the fact that the majority of people come to the show for a good day out. They come for the fun of saying that the 'Pig of the Year' reminds them of someone they know, or giggling at the idea of 'competitive waterfowl'. You can also have the pleasure of observing that BSE has not spoiled the pride of the owner of the winner of the Burke Cattle Championship; or of marvelling at the astonishing price of combine harvesters.

Almost half of those who attend do so every year. There is a ticket hotline (0121 767 4055), available from mid-January and there are discounts of as much as 25% if you book early enough, though it is not essential to do so. If you want to reserve a parking space, however, then you should do so well in advance. Prices are incredibly good value. Tickets for seats in the grandstand cannot be reserved in advance. There is free parking for up to 40,000 cars. No dogs are allowed but there is a crèche for children.

Although it is not primarily a horse show, there is an extensive equestrian programme. Most breeds are shown and there is top-class show jumping, while the magnificent heavy horses are always very popular.

Details are available from:
RASE, National Agricultural Centre, Stoneleigh Park,
Warwickshire CV8 2LZ
(Tel: 01203 696969).
Visit also the Royal Show website:
(www.royalshow.org.uk) or RASE website: (www.rase.org.uk).

Other Agricultural Shows

Other popular shows include the Three Counties Show, the Royal Cornwall Show, the Great Yorkshire Show, the Royal Norfolk Show, the East of England Show and the South of England Show.

The Royal Welsh Show and the Royal Highland Show are effectively the national agricultural shows for Wales and Scotland respectively. Of course there are many others. You may wish to dress tidily and will see traditionalists and local grandees in smart summer dresses as well as men in suits and ties. However, for many, this is an informal family day out and unless you have been invited to lunch in a smart enclosure you can relax. It is not necessary to book ahead and shows are good value, having a vast range of entertainment on offer. *Horse & Hound* and *The Field* magazines are good sources for show dates.

The British Grand Prix

The British Grand Prix has been held at Silverstone, Northamptonshire, since the mid-1980s. Formula One is now a multibillion dollar global sport and therefore the event has a great significance to the track that holds the event. Before then it was held on alternate years at Brands Hatch in Kent. Brands is hoping to see a return to F1 in 2002, although there is still some uncertainty about the details.

The British Grand Prix is the premier motor racing event in Britain and is usually held on the second Sunday of July. Advance booking for the grandstands begins in April and, with a capacity of 180,000 you can usually obtain tickets, but, as with so many events, do not leave it too late.

In the past all the great drivers have competed there, including Jim Clark and Graham Hill. The latter won the Daily Express International Trophy in a BRM in 1962 in what became known as a 'Silverstone finish'. The circuit's famous Woodcote corner (now made slower than it was in Hill's day) allows the possibility of overtaking and gaining the lead just before the finish. Sadly, Graham Hill died young in a plane crash and did not see his son Damon, who is now retiring, take the World Championship.

Racing began at Silverstone in 1948 when the disused airport hosted the RAC Grand Prix. In 1950 King George VI and Queen Elizabeth watched the legendary Juan Manuel Fangio race there, his first appearance in Britain. Since 1952 the track has been run by the British Racing Drivers Club (BRDC), who actually bought it in 1971, improving both the safety standards and the facilities for spectators.

The event itself is enormously popular which means dreadful traffic jams, so much so that many of the more affluent now choose to fly in. In fact there were over 3000 air movements at Silverstone for the Grand Prix in 1992 (around 90,000 people attended in 1998) and it is the busiest weekend of the year for helicopter taxi services. There is now an exclusive charity ball given on the Friday before the big race which many of the drivers and racing celebrities attend. This confirms the trend of many one day events expanding into entire weekend happenings.

General information from
Silverstone Racing Circuit, Northamptonshire
(Tel: 01327 857271, www.silverstone-circuit.co.uk).

Cricket

Cricket matches are really sporting occasions without much of a social side, except at the highest and lowest levels. Village cricket and its cousin, country-house cricket, are very much a part of the social season at a local and private level. As such, they are certainly a quintessential part of the summer scene. Driving through counties like Hampshire and Surrey in the summer there still seems to be cricket being played on almost every village green, with its attendant rituals of tea and then drinks in the local pub. Traditional house parties are often planned when a side from a big country house takes on a village eleven. Stories abound of the local blacksmith clean bowling a guest batsman before he has had time to acquaint himself with the horrendous state of the local pitch. One country landowner I knew managed to pursuade Imran Khan, the former captain of Pakistan, to join his side one year. The talented side were soundly thrashed by the villagers, a cause of great hilarity and many drinks all round.

County cricket is popular and Test Matches are major international events. However, cricket overall does not have that garden-party element which would make certain games a true part of the social season.

Lord's

Cricket at Lord's is, however, very much a part of the season for many. Fans include Mick Jagger and Sir Paul Getty, the philanthropist, who also hosts exclusive matches at his own home in Buckinghamshire. Former Prime Minister John Major is also a keen spectator, although he prefers the Oval to Lord's.

Cricket had already been played for 200 years when Thomas Lord was born at Thirsk in Yorkshire in 1755. His family had taken the losing side by supporting the Jacobites in 1745 when Bonnie Prince Charlie tried to regain the throne from his Hanoverian cousins. Young Thomas Lord went to London and made his fortune as a wine merchant. In his spare time, he made a name for himself as a ground bowler at the White Conduit Cricket Club in Islington. There he met the Earl of Winchelsea and Charles Lennox, later the 4th Duke of Richmond, who persuaded him to find a suitable site for the game in Marylebone. The first Lord's Cricket Ground was at Dorset Fields and Middlesex played Essex there in 1787. What became the Marylebone Cricket Club (MCC) took over from the Hambledon Cricket Club in Hampshire and they set about revising the laws of cricket. By the turn of the century, it was well established.

Not long afterwards the old Lord's became the site of a fixture which still continues today, the Eton and Harrow Cricket Match, which is usually played at the end of June. An early Harrow team included the poet Lord Byron. The match is still an enjoyable social occasion although it does not have the same significance that it did in the earlier years of the 20th century. Then team captains would be presented to the King after the match, which would have been attended as a matter of course by the Prime Minister, members of the Cabinet and members of the House of Lords. The young men in the teams then were seen as automatic leadership material of the future.

Back to the 18th century – Thomas Lord was forced to move from Dorset Fields to Regent's Park when his landlord put up the rent. However, when the canal was constructed it dissected his site causing him to move operations to the present site north west of Regent's Park in St John's Wood. There, theoretically there is still plenty of room, though the famous Long Room, part of the Pavilion, which was built in 1890, was designed to hold a MCC membership of 4000. There are now upwards of 18,000 members and there is a 15-year waiting list. In 1998 women were finally granted permission to become members. To join you would need to be proposed by an existing member and accepted by the committee. Players for the side may have their applications accelerated.

Guests of the MCC are entertained in a marquee in the Harris Garden. There are also some very comfortable new private boxes, for which members of the MCC can put their names into a ballot. Other stands include the Warner Stand, with 3000 seats, named after the great cricketer Sir Pelham Warner. The Grand Stand is an older building and has the scoreboard in the middle. On top of the scoreboard is the weathervane, known as Old Father Time, the only part of Lord's to have been damaged by bombing during the Second World War. The Father Time Boxes have their own private dining rooms at the back. At the far end of the ground, opposite the Pavilion, are the more modern stands, opened in 1991 and named after Denis Compton and Bill Edrich. Compton and Edrich were two brilliant Middlesex and England batsmen who scored over 3000 runs in 1947 and cheered up post-War Britain.

Lord's is officially the home ground of both Middlesex and England, as well as the MCC. It is possible to join the Middlesex County Cricket Club, which can be a good way of obtaining seats at Lord's, though it does not entitle members to use the Pavilion on international days.

The new stands at the Nursery End were named after the plant nursery which used to grow tulips on the site. The next stand is the New Mound, rebuilt in 1987, to commemorate the bicentenary of the MCC. Sir Paul Getty was a major contributor to the work, having been converted to cricket by Mick Jagger of the Rolling Stones, also a great fan of the game.

Finally, in the south-west corner is the Tavern Stand, which contains a very popular bar and some hospitality boxes. There is also a banqueting suite that can be used for entertaining when there is no cricket on. The famous Tavern pub is open all year round and visitors can also enter the MCC Museum and Library.

The first ever Test Match was held in Australia in 1877. The famous Ashes though came into being after Australia beat England at the Oval in 1882 (it was at Lord's in 1884 that England beat Australia by an innings). At the time this was a shock and before an age when England were used to being beaten by almost everyone. A spoof obituary written by Mr Shirley Brooks, son of the editor of *Punch*, appeared in the *Sporting Times*, announcing the death of English cricket and saying that its ashes had been taken to Australia. An English team then set off for Australia to win the Ashes back. They duly won two matches out of three and a Miss Florence Rose burned one of the bails and presented its Ashes in an urn to the captain of England, the Hon Ivo Bligh, whom she later married. After his death she sent Ashes and Urn to the MCC and they are still kept at Lord's regardless of whether England or Australia are the current holders.

For further information contact the
MCC Club Office
(Tel: 020 7289 1611, www.lords.org).

Other Cricket Venues

Apart from Lord's, Test cricket is also played at the Oval in South London, Trent Bridge in Nottingham, Old Trafford in Manchester, Headingley in Leeds and Edgbaston in Birmingham. There are also one-day internationals and, of course, county cricket matches during the summer season when village cricket also takes place.

Golf

The British Open

The British Open Golf Championship is held in mid-July but on different courses in England and Scotland. Scotland is of course the birthplace of golf, with records at the Royal and Ancient Golf Club in St Andrews dating back to 1754. The game today is enormously popular at all levels and more fashionable than it ever has been, with the expansion of the women's game having exceeded all expectations. As one of the world's four 'majors' alongside the US PGA Championship, the US Open and the Augusta Masters, the level of prize money is simply enormous. The Open is very popular and it is advisable to book early. You can obtain tickets from January and there are discounts offered for early booking. Secure a car parking place at the same time and book accommodation. The local tourist office should be able to help.

Other Golf Events

During the year there are various charity golf days held, sometimes taking the form of pro-am matches. These can be very social. Prince Andrew, the Duke of York, has taken part in one at Wentworth in Surrey.

There are also matches which are part of the European Tour such as the Benson & Hedges International Open and the Volvo PGA Championship in May and the British Masters in September.

For further information
(Tel: 01344 842881) –
European Tour Office for all golf information.

Conservancy & Game Fairs

The Game Fair

The Country Landowners Association (CLA) Game Fair, held in late July in the park of a large stately home, is the flagship event of the CLA. It is attended by well over 100,000 people each year, many of whom are not landowners but most of whom are interested in country life and country sports such as shooting and fishing. (It is not such a major event for the hunting fraternity.)

The Game Fair is quite a young event, having first been held in 1958, with the expressed aim of helping shooting enthusiasts re-establish their sport after the War. Two thousand visitors were expected and 8000 attended. It has gone on growing ever since and the concept has spread.

It moves to a different site each year. In 1999 it was held at Harewood House near Leeds but it has been held at Stratfield Saye in Hampshire, Cornbury Park near Oxford and on many other large estates which have the capacity to host such an event. Over 500 acres of grassland is required and, if this land is normally cultivated, it will take time for it to be reseeded and settle. Traffic jams en route to the Game Fair are as bad as any, rivalling the British Grand Prix and Badminton Horse Trials. It is also worth noting that most locations are not well served by trains and public transport. What's more the Game Fair is a shopping spree for many and they need their cars to carry off the loot. The best advice as ever is to go early or perhaps quite late. The Friday is a little less busy than the weekend.

Apart from grassland the hosts have to offer at least 1000 feet of good, open riverbank, for the fishing. The criteria for CLA selection include an area of at least 400×1000 yards free of public footpaths and other hazards for clay-pigeon shooting, which makes it a tall order to find a site. The landowner and everyone who works for the Game Fair will try to make certain the event breaks even, but it is a non-profit-making exercise.

A large part of its purpose is education. Over half those who attend live in cities and the idea is to demonstrate the part field sports play, both in the commercial life of the countryside and as leisure activities. A vital part of the message, apart from skill, safety, and sportsmanship, is conservation. Without conservation, there would be no countryside for the wildlife and thus no sport. Harder to grasp at first is the corollary that without sport, which brings in income, there would be less undeveloped countryside. A wood kept for shooting is less likely to be sold by the landowner for building. Shooting leads to the immediate death of the quarry involved but it also helps many species by preserving habitat and controlling vermin.

The Game Conservancy Trust, which always takes a stand at the Game Fair, is a leading body for the study of game and conservation. Modern issues concerning conservancy are both complex and controversial but also very important. The English grey partridge and the wild red grouse are its chief concerns. Populations of both have been in decline for some time, as have the populations of songbirds such as skylarks and even sparrows. Pesticides, intensive agriculture, and autumn cultivation are all contributors to the problem. What is fascinating is how nature will succeed given half a chance. However, control is needed, and predators that feed on ground nesting birds need to be considered in the ecological equation. Modern gamekeepers do not kill all vermin the way they used to and there are strict rules in place to protect the birds. A huge help could be simply to leave an unsprayed, uncultivated headland, or strip, around the edge of a field. The insects will soon return and with them the songbirds and some game birds.

The Game Fair hosts a number of trade stands selling everything from the increasingly sought after off-road vehicles to country clothing and equipment. There is Gunmakers' Row where visitors will find famous gunsmiths such as Purdey. There is Fisherman's Row and every form of kit from lifetime guaranteed socks to dog baskets. It is a fairly male event but there are craft tents and cookery displays. Many people bring small children but, in my experience, they get hot and bored trailing round as the Game Fair takes place over such a large area. Bigger children do enjoy the displays of skills such as accurate fly casting and some of the animals such as the working gun dogs or ferrets. There are usually falconry displays as well and you can often have a go at archery or rifle shooting. Increasingly there are high-tech gadgets on offer for the man who has everything.

The CLA has a member's enclosure or marquee for committee members and their guests. There are other enclaves that are by invitation only, but by and large you do not need to be a member to turn up and see what is going on. You can always get tickets at the gate, though it may be a good idea to make enquiries about booking them in advance as there are sometimes benefits. The Game Fair is a relaxed, accessible occasion. It is certainly popular. Dress is casual but tidy, with jacket and tie if you are a guest in one of the marquees. Flat caps abound.

Other Types of Game Fair

Similar events are now held in many other countries. There are also separate Game Fairs in Scotland and Northern Ireland and many smaller local versions. The best source of information about such events is the monthly magazine *The Field*. This periodical carries a listings section with full details of all such events including those organised by the Game Conservancy Trust and the Countryside Alliance, as well as other rural and sporting events, such as polo and racing.

Cowes
Week

The summer season supposedly ends with Cowes Week, an international sailing event held during the first week in August on the Isle of Wight. Like so many of the season's events it has strong connections with certain members of the Royal Family, notably the Duke of Edinburgh and the Princess Royal, who have competed in the regatta as individuals. The Royal Yacht *Britannia* is, however, now moored in Scotland and is no longer to be found at her accustomed place in Cowes Roads. Her passing from active service has taken away some of the event's very special atmosphere. Sir Paul Getty's yacht *Talitha G* and other glamorous visitors have striven to provide an alternative focal point, but as beautiful as *Talitha G* is, *Britannia* is proving irreplaceable.

The sailing is of the highest class, though the Solent is not suitable for a competition like the America's Cup. The Admiral's Cup is held every other year, in odd-numbered years and the historic Fastnet Race starts from Cowes, also on alternate years. It can be a tricky area in which to race yachts but sailing there is incredibly popular and competitive. Shore life and the parties that take place every night are as lively as ever, in fact more so since the balls held at the various sailing clubs made an effort to become younger and more casual. An exception to this is the Royal Yacht Squadron Ball, which is still very grand and formal.

Rumour has it that Cowes received its ascendancy as the yachting capital of the world in the reign of Elizabeth I. However, official Royal patronage did not take place until 1820 when King George IV began to take an interest. The Royal Yacht Squadron itself was formed in 1833 and is still Britain's most establishment sailing club. Its members are entitled to wear the White Ensign on their boats, while everyone else, including naval ships, must make do with Red.

Queen Victoria made the Isle of Wight fashionable when she and Prince Albert took to spending time at Osborne House, near Cowes, which the Prince, a great moderniser, made their most-up-to-date home. It is open to the public all summer. It is very interesting to see that the Prince Consort seems to have been a pioneer of such mod cons as built-in wardrobes with sliding doors.

Victoria and Albert's son King Edward VII also enjoyed Cowes, though his preferred companions, yacht owning plutocrats, would not have been to the taste of his mother.

More recently the Duke of Edinburgh has sailed with Uffa Fox at Cowes. When Fox became commodore of the Royal Yacht Squadron in 1964, he asked the then Rear Commodore, Viscount Runciman, to set up what is now known as the Cowes Combined Clubs to run the regatta. This arrangement is still in force. Effectively it means that the various clubs based in Cowes work together, use one starting line and one set of sailing instructions for the week. The daily races are run from the Royal Yacht Squadron line, using their platform, with its distinctive red and white roof. The gun line on the sea front is made up of 22 cannons from the reign of King William IV, known as the sailor king.

Cowes social life veers from one extreme to the other. On one side is tea on the Squadron Lawn, with iced coffee and little sandwiches, which is sedate and requires tidy clothes, although it is now self service. On the other are the wild discos enjoyed by young crew members and their friends and camp followers. Cowes is awash with private parties, large and small, on and off boats. The grand finale is the spectacular Friday night fireworks.

Ocean racing is one of the most expensive sports in the world. It is undertaken only by privileged owners with professional crews who seem to collect very glamorous followers. However, although the big boats do come to Cowes, there are many races for smaller sailing boats that are well supported and call for high degrees of skill and competitiveness. Some classes are popular with local people, such as the traditional classes for Bembridge Redwings, elegant craft only seen in the Solent. Many of those who come to Cowes have holiday homes in sailing villages on the island, such as Yarmouth, Seaview or Bembridge, where they and their children will have learned to sail in dinghies. There is a certain amount of good-natured competitiveness between them all. Each will hold its own social events at club level both during Cowes Week and at village regattas later in August.

Dress in Cowes is formal for anything to do with the Squadron. Older members sometimes wear brown shoes with blue suits, a combination not normally associated with good taste. Other than this, dress is dictated by practicality, though it is noticeable that some of the most nautically dressed never go near a sailing boat. In Cowes itself are many shops which sell the most trendy sailing gear.

Cowes is accessible by ferry directly from Southampton and other car and passenger ferries run from Lymington to Yarmouth and Portsmouth to Ryde. There are hourly fast trains from Waterloo to Portsmouth. This route also has a crossing by hovercraft (hovercrafts were invented and developed on the island.) It is essential to book ahead at busy times such as Cowes Week and indeed during most of the school holidays. Accommodation in Cowes is scarce as it is not a very big town, so book ahead and consider staying inland, away from the better known areas. The centre of the island is still very unspoilt.

For further information contact the
Cowes Combined Clubs and Solent Cruising and Racing Association,
18 Bath Road, Cowes, Isle of Wight
(Tel: 01983 295744, www.cowesweek.co.uk)
or The Royal Yacht Squadron, The Castle, Cowes,
Isle of Wight PO31 7QT
(Tel: 01983 292191, www.rys.com).

Scotland

The Scottish social season takes place mainly in August and September. For many years The Royal Yacht Britannia would leave Cowes and head for Scotland, taking the Queen and the Royal Family for a Hebridean cruise en route to Balmoral. Once there, the family would spend most of August and September in Scotland. The season originated because the court followed the sovereign as he/she progressed from one palace to another. Some traces of this Royal progress are still visible in the modern season after Cowes Week when the focus moves, not only away from London, but away from the South altogether.

Of course nobody now goes to Scotland because the Royal Family does so. They go for various reasons including field sports. The grouse shooting season begins on the 12th August, with salmon fishing and deer stalking taking place in the late summer and autumn. Neither the salmon fishing nor the grouse shooting are what they once were. Numbers are down partly due to pressure on habitat and therefore prices are up. However, people are still drawn to the idea that, even if they are not going to shoot or fish, they can spend several weeks in the Highlands with their families renting lodges, staying with friends or in hotels, walking, picnicking or playing golf. There are also highland gatherings, the Highland Games and, of course, highland balls.

The Edinburgh International Festival

Culture is another draw, especially the Edinburgh International Festival and its Fringe events. The Festival has grown over the years and looks set to continue doing so. In 1994 the new Edinburgh Festival Theatre, (formerly the Empire Theatre) was opened. This houses major productions of opera and Shakespeare, as well as concerts and dance. The new theatre adds 2000 seats. It is a useful addition to the older venues as it allows more ambitious productions to be staged owing to its larger stage. This in turn has encouraged internationally renowned dance companies, who now have more space in which to perform. Dance plays a large part in the festival's more serious cultural side. Music too is central to the event and has been so since the beginning. Apart from the new theatre the major venues are the Queen's Hall, Usher Hall, the King's Theatre, the Edinburgh Playhouse and the Royal Lyceum Theatre.

As well as the performing arts there are exhibitions of paintings and sculpture. Among the major venues are the National Gallery of Scotland, the Scottish National Portrait Gallery, the Scottish Gallery of Modern Art, the Royal Museum of Scotland and the Assembly Rooms and there are at least another 30 venues.

In addition, there is a film festival, a biennial book festival, and a jazz festival. During the last three weeks of August there is also the Edinburgh Military Tattoo, which features massed pipes and drums from all over the world.

Almost better known than the Festival itself is the Fringe, where, in the 1960s, such luminaries as Alan Bennett, Peter Cook, Dudley Moore and Jonathan Miller first became well known. Since then it has been the route taken by many of their successors. It is a genuine home for fringe theatre where tiny productions (often in Latvian for some reason) and other comedy performances push the boundaries of taste and daring. The fun is spotting tomorrow's stars, although no one can manage to see everything and nor would they want to. Performances are mounted wherever there is a square inch of space and there are an increasingly overwhelming number. The Fringe programme is published in late June and may be obtained from the Edinburgh Festival Fringe, 180 High Street, Edinburgh EH1 1QS (Tel: 0131 226 5257 or 0131 226 5259).

The Festival itself was founded in 1947 with Queen Elizabeth as patron. It attracted many doubters at first, but now attracts visitors from all over the world, although 60% are from Scotland and indeed Edinburgh itself. It also continues to attract top international musicians and artists.

The city of Edinburgh is obviously very busy during the Festival so either book ahead or be flexible. There are plenty of places to stay if you give matters some thought.

Edinburgh Tourist Advice (Tel: 0131 557 9655) will help with information on where to stay. The Edinburgh International Festival Office is at 21 Market Street, Edinburgh EH1 1BW (Tel: 0131 473 2001, www.edinburghfestivals. co.uk). Here you may also enquire about becoming a 'Friend', always well worthwhile as you will receive priority booking and other benefits such as invitations to private views.

Scottish Games

The Edinburgh Festival always takes place in August. In September the Braemar Royal Highland Gathering is held further north, near Aberdeen on Royal Deeside and the Queen and other members of the Royal Family often attend. It is said that Kenneth McAlpine, first King of the Scots had his hunting box there. King Malcolm Canmore would call the clans to the Braes of Mar to select the hardiest soldiers and fleetest messengers by making them compete in games. The ruins of Malcolm's 11th century stronghold, Kindrochit Castle, are still to be seen.

In 1715 the Earl of Mar raised the standard for the exiled James III (The Old Pretender) and began the first Jacobite rising. After the failure of the second rising, in 1745, when James's son Bonnie Prince Charlie (The Young Pretender), had seriously rattled his Hanoverian cousin George by invading England, things Scottish went out of fashion in a big way. Indeed, Highland dress was even made illegal for some years.

However, Queen Victoria developed a strong taste for tartan, and became patron of the Braemar Gathering in 1848. Her presence supported the Braemar Highland Society, a body whose aims were to preserve the kilt and indeed the language and culture of the Highlands. What the Queen and the Royal Family see now when they attend the gathering is pretty much what Queen Victoria would have witnessed.

There is Highland dancing, tossing the caber, putting the stone, throwing the hammer, sprinting and the quaintly named long leap. In addition there is an inter-services tug-of-war and a relay race. The games usually start at around 9.30a.m. and finish around 5p.m.

The gathering is held at the Princess Royal and Duke of Fife Memorial Park at Braemar. The Queen is patron and her cousin the Duke of Fife, whose forebears gave the 12-acre ground to the society in 1906, is one of three vice-patrons. It is possible to book tickets in advance and advisable if you want grandstand tickets, which sell out very early. You should apply in writing to: The Bookings Secretary, BRHS, Coilacriech, Ballater, Aberdeenshire AB35 5UH. (Tel: 013397 55377). Those who turn up on the day will not get a grandstand seat but the hills and terraces offer good views. Many people from all over the world attend and the competitors too come from far afield. There is plenty of accommodation but the best is booked up early. The Area Tourist Office is on Bridge Street, Banchory, Kincardineshire AB31 5SX (Tel: 01330 822000). They will send you a list if you enclose a stamped, addressed envelope.

Apart from such events as the Highland Games, which make a day out, much of the social life of the Scottish season revolves around sport and takes place in private houses. Gatherings centre around such events as the early autumn race meetings at Perth and of course dances. Most of the latter are a combination of by-invitation and ticket purchase. They are not the type of event you can simply turn up to without knowing anyone. Cognoscenti will tell you that the Skye Balls are the most fun and that the Perth Ball is the smartest and most formal. The Northern Meeting is held in and around Inverness at various venues. Although Scottish dancing is for all ages, the balls are predominantly the playground of hearty singles in their twenties. If you live in London and are interested in learning to reel your best bet is to contact Toby Trustram Eve on 0956 386334. He organises reeling classes.

Charity Events

The early autumn sees the season coming back to London. In the old days this period was called the Little Season and ran from October until Christmas, the idea being that by then people were back from their summer holidays in Scotland or elsewhere. The outdoor, summer season is replaced by the busiest time of the year for charity events, gallery openings, book launches, charity fairs and, in the run up to Christmas itself, charity carol concerts.

The vast majority of charity balls are run along similar lines. A chairman (usually a woman) will gather a committee, each of whom will aim to fill a table of ten. Thus a committee of 30 people should generate 300 people. Committee members might also be asked to find prizes for tombolas, raffles or auctions. They will also help organise the décor or suggest celebrities who might be able to attend, which in turn will help with sponsorship.

The usual schedule for a big charity ball in a London hotel would be a champagne reception, followed by a seated dinner. After dinner there might be speeches by those involved with the charity, or an auction, or perhaps a cabaret of some kind. At the Anglo-Brazilian Ball, for instance, there is usually a performance by dancers from Rio. Dancing will follow, usually to a live band in the ballroom. The whole evening will run from 8.30p.m. to, say, one or two in the morning. Many older guests will leave early. Those who can afford it may pay for an entire table of ten and invite their friends as guests. Others must diplomatically invite their friends saying it will cost them £75 a head or whatever the figure is. If your ticket has been paid for by your host, good manners dictate that you should spend lavishly on raffle tickets or whatever else is on offer. After-dinner auctions, at which 'big-ticket' items such as holidays in the Maldives may be on offer, are usually aimed at the high rollers present. Any money made is pure profit for the charity. If you are asked on to a committee and can bring a very rich friend who will bid in the auction you will be popular indeed. There are dances aimed at a younger age group such as the plethora of teenage parties in the Christmas holidays or those such as the White Knights' Ball, held just after the New Year, where most people will be in their twenties or thirties. *Harpers & Queen* lists many of the balls in its April issue. Another good source of information is the *London and UK Datebook*, a quarterly magazine available on subscription, which aims to list all the major charity events and provide useful supplementary information (Tel: 020 7584 8462). The vast majority are black tie but big traditional ball dresses are not worn as universally as they once were and women are choosing both short dresses and the more informal long dresses, often worn with scarves or shawls. It is often possible to buy tickets for these events if you see them listed, but it is more usual to be sent ticket information by someone on the committee. Some balls are themed, like the War and Peace Ball, at which there is formal Russian dancing, or the Royal Caledonian or St Andrew's Balls which are, surprisingly enough, Scottish in flavour. Some do have the feel of a private party with most people known to one another, but most are open to any supporter of the charity who would like to contribute to its aims in this way. Ticket prices vary but very few tickets are now under £50 or £60 a head and some are much more, perhaps £250. However, we are still a long way from the American 'benefit' evenings where tickets may cost thousands of dollars.

If you support a particular charity such as Macmillan Cancer Relief or the NSPCC you can get details of their events from their offices. Macmillan, like many other big charities, has an outstanding Christmas fair, held in the horticultural halls in Vincent Square. These fairs are a good source of Christmas presents and usually charge an entrance fee. There are stalls which directly benefit the charity such as Macmillan Cancer Relief's well known Christmas card and decoration stall. Other stalls, selling anything from children's clothes, to hand-painted china, will have rented their space or agreed to give a percentage of what they earn directly to the charity. Such fairs are often highly social occasions, sometimes with an evening preview with drinks served. Many of the stalls sell items that would be hard to find in ordinary shops and they can be well worth visiting.

Of course there are other fundraising parties apart from balls, such as private views of exhibitions, auctions, opera nights, concerts and, nearer Christmas, carol concerts. Many of these are listed in the national press, others you may hear about through the charities themselves or through friends and of course the London churches at which they are held. The events calendar in Appendix VII of this book lists only London Christmas carol services but they are of course held all over the country and details of them can be found locally.

Of the charity balls aimed at teenagers, the best known is probably the Feathers, tickets for which always sell out incredibly early. The NSPCC and ICAN run others. Again, details may be found in *Harpers & Queen* and the *Datebook*. The balls are stewarded, but they can still be quite wild. Not surprisingly they are most popular with children who attend single-sex boarding schools.

National Hunt Racing

In November, the flat-racing season ends where it began, at Doncaster. The last big social race meeting will have been held at Newmarket a couple of weeks earlier. National Hunt racing (or the winter game as it is sometimes known) actually starts in the late summer but the first really big meeting which might be considered to be part of the social season is the Hennessy Cognac Gold Cup at Newbury in late November. Many also attend the early November meeting at Cheltenham, particularly the Countryside Race Day on the eve of the Murphy's Gold Cup.

National Hunt racing is less smart in some ways than flat racing in that any hat you may choose to wear should be there to keep you warm rather than for mere adornment. However, jump racing certainly has its social side. Among the highlights are the King George VI Gold Cup, a major steeplechase at Kempton Park on Boxing Day, and the Grand Military Cup at Sandown Park, a top race for amateur riders. The highpoint of the season is, however, the Cheltenham Festival, held over three days in March, which is effectively the Ascot of jump racing.

Cheltenham

As with Ascot, Cheltenham crowds are huge and it is essential to buy members' enclosure badges in advance. If you purchase tickets before December 31st there is usually a discount. They are available to all, though if you wish to attend more than just the big meeting it could be worth becoming a full annual member. Full annual membership brings added privileges such as admission to the County Stand, which is a good place from which to watch the racing. You may be lucky enough to be invited into someone's box or to the Turf Club marquee, which is a great base of operations, especially when it is very cold and wet. However, most will buy a daily member's badge, as there are ample facilities. The traffic can be terrible especially on Thursday, Gold Cup Day, so leave plenty of time.

The meeting is held over three days. Tuesday is Champion Hurdle day, Wednesday the Queen Mother Champion Chase and Thursday the Gold Cup itself, the most valuable steeple-chase in Europe.

Racing at Cheltenham began in 1819 on Cleeve Hill, which overlooks the modern racecourse at Prestbury Park. It has grown ever more popular since, partly due to the fact that the horses stay in training for several years and the public gets to know them. Cheltenham has spawned household names such as 'Arkle' and 'Desert Orchid', as well known as those of top sportsmen and women. 'Arkle' won the Gold Cup at Cheltenham three times in succession in 1964, 1965 and 1966. His statue is to be found at Cheltenham and there is also a race named after him. 'Arkle' was trained in Ireland, as many great winners at Cheltenham have been. Much of the great atmosphere at Cheltenham is provided by the annual 'invasion' of the Irish owners, trainers and racegoers. There is always a resounding cheer if an Irish horse wins.

Lately Cheltenham has become very fashionable and seems to attract a surprising number of people from the worlds of fashion, rock music and art, people more usually associated with trendy venues. However, they seem to love dressing in tweed and soaking up the wonderful atmosphere. Members of the Royal Family do attend, notably the Queen Mother for a number of years, but it is not a formal occasion. Having said that, men in the members' enclosure should wear a suit and tie. Many wear covert coats over their suits but some wear waxed cotton jackets. Tweeds look best for women, worn with flat-heeled boots and I still favour a skirt suit although trouser suits are allowed and many people wear them. Fake fur hats have had a long reign, replacing velvet berets, but stetsons seem to be taking over. Tea cosy shapes are not usually all that becoming, but whatever shape you choose the trick is to keep it simple – over the top feathered creations are not suitable. You should look quite smart; headscarves and wellington boots are more for point-to-points than Cheltenham. (Tel: 01242 513014, www. Cheltenham.co.uk.)

The Grand National

The Grand National, at Aintree Racecourse, is probably the best known race in the calendar but it is less of a social occasion than Cheltenham although it does have a unique atmosphere. The train is probably the best way of getting there from London. There are special trains laid on, so you can enjoy a late breakfast on the way there and dinner on the way back. You may also choose to stay in Liverpool itself. Traditionally the Adelphi Hotel was the centre of all the fun. The meeting lasts for three days and the quality of racing on the Thursday and the Friday has been greatly improved in recent years. This includes two races over the Grand National fences, notably the Foxhunters or 'amateur Grand National'. There are also some good races over the conventional park fences, known as the Mildmay Course, and high-class hurdle races too. On the Saturday many people bring cars and picnics and park by the Canal Turn, eating on rugs and out of the car boot. The view of the course is not brilliant but there are giant TV screens in place. Hearty types arrive early, pick a favourite spot and then walk the course. Standing on the landing side of Becher's Brook with the fence looming several feet above your head certainly makes you appreciate the courage of both riders and horses.

The fences were made safer in 1991, but this has in no way diminished the spectacle. Sadly, there have been many accidents and even fatalities during the race, which has prompted some interest from animal rights activists who think the event cruel. However, the majority of racehorses are greatly valued by their owners and live an enviable life.

The Whitbread Gold Cup

The last big event of the National Hunt season is the Whitbread Gold Cup at Sandown Park on the last Saturday in April, which is actually the only race meeting with flat and jumps on the same card.

Point-To-Points

Point-to-pointing is an amateur sport, whose season runs from January to late May. Local point-to-points are usually run for the benefit of the hunt and may be a major local social event. This is especially true if the area is quite remote, as the day becomes a focal point for the neighbourhood. The Heythrop and Beaufort point-to-points in Gloucestershire are among the smartest. It is never necessary, though usually possible, to get tickets in advance. Many people take picnics, which they serve from the backs of their four-wheel drive vehicles and the strategic parking places are snapped up early by those in the know. Otherwise, you can usually become a day member. Priority is given to farmers whose land the hunt rides over during the hunting season. There may be a special marquee for members and guests. Dress is dictated by common sense but scruffiness is not correct at any horsy event and muted country colours are preferred to garish waterproofs. Most point-to-points are at weekends and people bring their children.

Point to Point Information:
Horse and Hound Magazine
(Tel: 020-7261-6315).

The London International Boat Show

The London International Boat Show is held at Earl's Court over 11 days in January. The Boat Show has become one of the biggest events of its type in the world. The first day is a preview but tickets are available in advance. Otherwise you can purchase a ticket on the door. Inside you can buy anything you need from wet-suits to jet skis, canoes, or an ocean going yacht. Much of the clothing and equipment on sale is cheaper than it would be at an ordinary chandler and a lot of what is unveiled at the show is state of the art. Sailing boats are displayed alongside power boats, motor boats and all the latest technology.

Boat Show Information:
The British Motorboat Industry Federation
(Tel: 01784 473377, www.bmif.co.uk).

The
Boat Race

The Oxford *v* Cambridge Boat Race is very much a part of the season for some. It is one of those quintessentially English annual events which has a life of its own. People will ask who won the Boat Race, or say they support the Dark Blues (Oxford) or Light Blues (Cambridge), yet never think about rowing as a sport from one year to the next. It takes place in late March or early April on the River Thames between Putney and Mortlake, where the river is tidal, which can make a big difference, as can other conditions such as the wind and currents. Strategy is balanced by brute strength.

The event dates back to 1829 and so far there has only been one dead heat, in 1877. The course is four and a quarter miles long and runs from Putney Bridge, upstream round a long bend in the river to Mortlake. Because of the bend it matters which side you are allotted. The north is called the Middlesex station and the south the Surrey station; a coin is flipped to see which team is allocated to which station.

The race itself takes around 20 minutes. The time may vary from year to year. The teams are made up of eight oarsmen and a cox. The rowers are all men but recently there have been several women coxes. The teams are all amateurs and must be currently studying at one of the universities. Nowadays, many of them are post-graduates in their twenties, often Americans or other nationalities, who in many cases are very experienced, destroying some of the gentlemanly amateurish spirit of the event. In the past there would have been a good quota of Old Etonians, Radleyans and former grammar school boys of 19 or 20 who had rowed for their schools and made the effort to train while also working towards their final examinations. The training methods are much more professional than they were in the Boat Race's golden age. The design of the boats and the oars used is frequently updated. Nevertheless, it remains a Corinthian event which demands enormous heart from those who take part. They still compete purely for the glory of winning a Blue, or university colour, which remains a great honour.

The training is time consuming and exhausting, and months of work on the water may only win a place in one of the reserve boats, Goldie for Cambridge, or Isis for Oxford. For the few weeks leading up to the event you will receive a small amount of press coverage as a team member. During the gruelling race itself, you will be seen on television all over the world, but that's about it. Of course some team members will go on to take part in the Olympic Games or may row in the Boat Race for a second year, but for most it truly represents Andy Warhol's 'fifteen minutes of fame'.

To watch the Boat Race live you can secure a free place on the tow path on either side of the river. To get a place in one of the launches which follow the teams you need to be a member or guest of the Victoria League or the Oxford and Cambridge University Boat Club. Dress for warmth above all. Many people have a pub lunch before the race but the most popular watering holes get very crowded. In most years there is a Boat Race Ball in the evening. (www.archive. comlab.ox.ac.uk/other/rowing/ox-cam.html).

Conclusion

Anyone attending all the events listed in this book would have little time to do anything else. It is surprising in some ways that so many still take place during the week, sometimes for several days running, and yet attract vast crowds. Perhaps these events are the equivalent of the Saint's days and Fiestas held in more Mediterranean climes. A great many are held outdoors in spite of the fickle weather, and many involve picnicking while dressed formally, which can be quite tricky, though only Henley and Ascot maintain their specific dress codes.

Many people see the season as exclusive and in some way not for them. This is quite untrue as any visit to an event will soon make clear. It may turn out not to be your sort of thing but no one will try to exclude you any more. Others believe that it has become too commercial with sponsorship, corporate entertainment, and bolted-on celebrities. I personally think that it is one of the things we do best in this country. Almost all the events listed are both accessible and enjoyable; with a little know-how, they are well worth experiencing live rather than watching on television. Of course, there is commercial sponsorship, though not at either Royal Ascot or Henley and of course corporate entertainment is a fact of life, but I do not consider this to be a problem. In fact, for many of the headline events, corporate packages are the best method of gaining access and watching them in comfort. If you do feel that the bigger events have been ruined then there is a plethora of smaller ones, especially outside London, which still have plenty of atmosphere.

The season is something to celebrate, so break out the champagne, put the picnic hamper in the boot, remember all the badges and car park passes, and off you go.

Appendix I

Various Booking Requirements

Events Listed 'Booking Essential'

For those events marked 'advance booking essential' book at least three months in advance or see individual entries for requirements. For most arts events it would be worth becoming a 'friend' and obtaining priority booking facilities. Enquire about mailing lists. Do this as many months ahead as possible.

Wimbledon

To be included in the ballot for Wimbledon apply by December at the latest the preceding year. Otherwise plan from January for May and June and enquire about booking tickets or membership.

Appendix II

Applications for Royal Ascot

Applications to the Royal Enclosure

The Ascot Office is open from January until April. There is always a notice of this in the press. Those wishing to apply should study the conditions stated, as these may vary slightly from one year to the next.

Those applying for vouchers to the Royal Enclosure for the first time should have their requests in by the end of March. There is absolutely no appeal if you miss the deadline and no exceptions are ever made, so do not forget to organise yourself in good time if you want to attend. However, there are no longer restrictions as to who may apply, as there were in the past, such as no divorcees. In the unlikely event that your correctly completed application is not accepted, no explanation will be given. An acknowledgement will be sent to you if your application is successful.

Vouchers are free (you pay for them when you exchange them for your badges) and applying for one does not commit you to anything, but without a voucher, entry to the Royal Enclosure is impossible. You may exchange the voucher, which must be signed, at the Ascot Office itself, by post in advance, or at one of two special entrances on the racecourse itself. The latter does not take long and it is the most sensible, in case of a sudden change of plan. If you come on more than one day keep your badge then hand it in and get a new daily one the next day. It does not matter if you leave a gap, say going on Tuesday and then Friday, but it does matter if you lose the badge. Alternatively, you may purchase a four day badge which is usually slightly better value.

Your badge is your entry ticket to the whole racecourse, not just the enclosure. However, car parking is separate and any extra badges such as tickets for White's Club or the Jockey Club or even a box only give entry to those areas, not the Royal Enclosure. Therefore, apply for vouchers even if you know you will be a guest in a private marquee or box. You must wear your name badge at all times and they are strictly non-transferable.

First-Timers

Those applying for the first time need to be sponsored by someone who has been present in the Royal Enclosure for at least eight years. You may only sponsor two people in any one year. Sponsorship forms are available from the Ascot Office, St James's Palace, London SW1A 1BP and should be requested before the voucher application is sent off. First timers may be restricted as to their choice of day, probably to Friday only. This will apply for one year after which they can apply for a voucher that can be exchanged for any or all the four days of the meeting.

The Wording of a Voucher Application

A request for a voucher application is traditionally worded in the third person as follows:

> *Mr John Smith presents his compliments to Her Majesty's Representative and wishes to apply for vouchers to the Royal Enclosure for his wife Mrs John Smith (children's names where applicable) and himself.*

Your address should be at the top. Headed writing paper is best. The letter should be dated bottom right. (See also *Debrett's Correct Form.*) Children's ages should be included if they are between 16 and 25 years old. There are concessions for people under 30. Children under 16 are *not allowed* in the Royal Enclosure. You may not apply on behalf of friends. Visitors with overseas passports should apply to their own ambassadors or high commissioners. The Ascot Office will answer procedural queries only.

Booking 'Other' Tickets in Advance

It is essential to book tickets in advance for areas other than the Royal Enclosure, as these are very popular. For all enquiries other than applications for vouchers for the Royal Enclosure, including car parking, contact Ascot Racecourse, Ascot, Berkshire SL5 7JN (Tel: 01344 876876).

Dress Codes

Dress in the Royal Enclosure is restricted to morning suits and top hats or service dress for men, and formal day dress with a hat which covers the crown of the head for women. Those deemed incorrectly dressed will be turned away.

Appendix III

Clothing Suppliers

Women's Clothes – Made to Measure

- Laura B Couture, 8 Yeoman's Row, London SW3 2AH (Tel: 020 7581 4123)

Laura Benjamin dresses women in the know who need to attend a great many social events and fully understands their requirements. She sells both ready-to-wear and made-to-measure clothes. She also has a collection of hats in the same fabrics for a fully co-ordinated look. Her prices are at the top of the range but, with her, you will avoid expensive mistakes.

- Philippa May, Hartforth Mill, Gilling West, Richmond, North Yorkshire DL10 5JZ (Tel: 01748 823176)

Philippa May works from home but shows her collections in spring and autumn at Newmarket and Berkshire, as well as London and Yorkshire. Ring for details. She specialises in dresses and matching coats and suits suitable for all occasions of the season, of which she has an insider's knowledge. You can choose from her collection and then have garments made to order.

Women's Designers

- Tomasz Starzewski, 177 Sloane Street, London SW1X 9QL (Tel: 020 7235 4526)

He is one the best designers of clothes for the season. His trademark ultra-smart suits come with jackets of varying lengths and he now stocks bags and hats. He is also strong on luxurious evening wear.

- Caroline Charles, 56-57 Beauchamp Place, London SW3 1NY (Tel: 020 7225 3197)

Her feminine, flattering clothes are easy to wear and fashionable, understated but perfect for the job. Her collections tend to evolve and can last for many seasons.

Stores and the High Street

- Debenhams, Oxford Street, and branches.

- Fenwick, in Bond Street – good hats and accessories.

- Selfridges, Oxford Street, has been revamped with a big range, personal shopping which can help co-ordinate an outfit and has good hair and beauty salon.

- Jigsaw, best of the high street multiples, good quality suits.

- Karen Millen is recommended to the young and thin.

- Monsoon and its sister business Accessorize can be happy hunting grounds.

Men's Clothes – Made to Measure

- Bernard Weatherill, 8 Savile Row, London W1X 1AF (Tel: 020 7734 6905)

- Gieves & Hawkes, 1 Savile Row, London W1X 2JR (Tel: 020 7434 2001)

Men's Clothes – Ready to Wear

- Oliver Brown, 75 Lower Sloane Street, London SW1W 8DA (Tel: 020 7259 9494)

- Hackett, 31-32 King Street, Covent Garden, London WC2E 8JD (Tel: 020 7240 2040 and branches)

Men's Formal and Hire

- Moss Bros, 88 Regent Street, London W1R 5PA (Tel: 020 7494 0666 and branches)

Hatters

- John Boyd, 16 Beauchamp Place SW3 1NQ (Tel: 020 7589 7601)

- Frederick Fox, 87 New Bond Street, London W1Y 9LA (Tel: 020 7629 5706)

- Graham Smith, 22 Crawford Street, London W1H 1TJ (Tel: 020 7935 5625)

- Philip Treacy, 69 Elizabeth Street, London SW1 W9PJ (Tel: 020 7259 9605)

Appendix IV

Places to Stay for Events

Some are not the nearest but all are top class and welcome international visitors:

Home Counties

- Cliveden House, Cliveden, Taplow, Maidenhead, Berkshire SL6 0JF (Tel: 01628 668561) for Ascot, Henley, the Royal Windsor Horse Show and polo at Guards

Midlands

- Lygon Arms, Broadway, Worcestershire WR12 7DU (Tel: 01386 852255) for Cheltenham, Badminton and the Royal Show

- Hambleton Hall Hotel, Hambleton, nr Oakham, Rutland LE15 8TH (Tel: 01572 756991) for Burghley Horse Trials

North East

- Britannia Adelphi Hotel, Ranelagh Place, Liverpool L3 5UL (Tel: 0151 709 7200) for the Grand National

- The Chester Grosvenor Hotel, Eastgate, Chester CH1 1LT (Tel: 01244 324024) for Chester races

South

- The Angel Hotel, North Street, Midhurst, West Sussex GU29 9DN (Tel: 01730 812421)

- Spread Eagle Hotel, South Street, Midhurst, West Sussex GU29 9NH (Tel: 01730 816911)

- Marriott Goodwood Park Hotel and Country Club, Goodwood, Chichester, West Sussex PO18 0QB (Tel: 01243 775537) for Goodwood Races and Festival of Speed, Hickstead, Cowdray Park Polo and Glyndebourne

- The Priory Bay Hotel, Priory Drive, Seaview, Isle of Wight PO34 5BU (Tel: 01983 613146) for Cowes Week

Scotland

- Gleneagles Hotel, Auchterarder, Perthshire PH3 1NF (Tel: 01764 662231)

- The Balmoral, 1 Princes Street, Edinburgh EH2 2EQ (Tel: 0131 556 2414)

The North

- Middlethorpe Hall Hotel, Bishopthorpe Road, York YO23 2GB (Tel: 01904 641241) for York Races, Harrogate Flower Show, Doncaster Races

Wales

- Llangoed Hall, Llyswen, Brecon, Powys, Wales LD3 0YP (Tel: 01874 754525) for Royal Welsh Show, Hay-on-Wye Literary Festival

East Anglia

- The Rutland Arms Hotel, High Street, Newmarket, Suffolk CB8 8NB (Tel: 01638 664251) for Newmarket Races.

Appendix V
Food & Catering

Hampers

- Beverley Hills Bakery, 3 Egerton Terrace, London SW3 2BX (Tel: 020 7584 4401)
- Fortnum and Mason, 181 Piccadilly, London W1A 1ER (Tel: 020 7734 8040)
- Partridges of Sloane Street, 132-134 Sloane Street, London SW1X 9AT (Tel: 020 7730 7102)

Some event organisers also provide picnic services. Many have tied-in picnics – you simply arrive and can pick up a pre-ordered picnic. Others can recommend local providers.

Caterers and Party Organisers

- The Admirable Crichton, Unit 6, Camberwell Trading Estate, Denmark Road, London SE5 9LB (Tel: 020 7733 8113)
- Bentley's Entertainments, 7 Square Rigger Row, Plantation Wharf, London SW11 3TZ (Tel: 020 7223 7900)
- Fait Accompli, Unit 1, 39 Tadema Road, London SW10 0PZ (Tel: 020 7352 2777)
- William Bartholemew Party Organizing, 18 The Talina Centre, Bagleys Lane, London SW6 2BW (Tel: 020 7731 8328)
- Gardner Merchant, Manor House, Manor Farm Road, Alperton, Middlesex HA0 1BN (Tel: 020 8566 9222)
- Ring & Brymer, Manor House, Manor Farm Road, Alperton, Middlesex HA0 1BN (Tel: 020 8566 9222)
- Letherby & Christopher, Mayfair House, Belvue Road, Northolt, Middlesex UB5 5QJ (Tel: 020 8357 3000)

- Payne & Gunter, Mayfair House, Belvue Road, Northolt, Middlesex UB5 5QJ (Tel: 020 8842 2224)
- Mustard, 1-3 Brixton Road, London SW9 6DE (Tel: 020 7840 5900)

Appendix VI

Health Farms, Spas & Beauty

- Ragdale Hall, Ragdale Village, Melton Mowbray, Leicestershire LE14 3PB (Tel: 01664 434831)

- Shrublands Hall Health Clinic, Coddenham, Suffolk IP6 9QH (Tel: 01473 830404)

- Henlow Grange, Henlow, Bedfordshire SG16 6DB (Tel: 01462 811111)

- Chewton Glen Hotel, Christchurch Road, New Milton, Hampshire BH25 6QS (Tel: 01425 275341)

Appendix VII
Calendar of Events

<table>
<tr><td>January</td><td></td></tr>
<tr><td></td><td>London International Boat Show
Location: Earls Court Exhibition Centre, London
Contact Details: 01784 473377</td></tr>
<tr><td>Mid Jan</td><td>Salmon Fishing Season Starts
Notes: Check local river seasons in each area</td></tr>
<tr><td></td><td>Point-to-Point Season Starts
Notes: Horse and Hound magazine is a good source for point-to-point information</td></tr>
<tr><td>Jan/Feb</td><td>The Watercolours and Drawings Fair
Location: Park Lane Hotel, London
Contact Details: 020 7439 2822</td></tr>
<tr><td>31st</td><td>End of Shooting Season</td></tr>
<tr><td>February</td><td></td></tr>
<tr><td>15th</td><td>The Red & Sika Hind Season Closes
Location: Scotland</td></tr>
<tr><td>15th</td><td>The Roe & Fallow Doe Season Closes
Location: Scotland</td></tr>
<tr><td></td><td>6 Nations Rugby Commences
Location: England, Ireland, Scotland, Wales, France, Italy
Notes: Usual ticket allocation to rugby clubs and schools. Hospitality packages may be available though
Contact Details: 020 8892 2000</td></tr>
<tr><td></td><td>Olympia Fine Art and Antiques Spring Fair
Location: Olympia, Hammersmith Road, London W14
Contact Details: 020 7373 8141 Tickets, 020 7385 1200 General information</td></tr>
<tr><td></td><td>Royal Horticultural Society Spring Flower Shows
Location: Royal Horticultural Halls, Westminster, London
Notes: These run until April and are a must for the serious gardener
Contact Details: 020 7630 7422</td></tr>
</table>

28th	The Red & Sika Hind Season Closes *Location: England & Wales*
28th	The Roe & Fallow Doe Season Closes *Location: England & Wales*
March	

Crufts Dog Show
Location: National Exhibition Centre, Birmingham
Notes: Advanced booking advised if interested in a
specific class although not essential
Contact Details: Box Office: 020 7518 1012
Kennel Club: 0870 606 6750

Chelsea Antiques Fair
Location: Chelsea Old Town Hall, Kings Rd,
London SW3
Contact Details: 01444 482514

BADA Antiques and Fine Arts Fair
Location: Duke of York's Headquarters, Kings Rd,
London, SW3
Contact Details: 020 7589 6108

Grand Military Cup
Location: Sandown Racecourse
Notes: An event for amateur riders with service contacts
Contact Details: 01372 470047

National Hunt Festival
Location: Cheltenham Racecourse
Notes: Book by Dec 31 for discounts and well ahead for
members' enclosure
Contact Details: 01242 513014

Flat Racing Season Begins
Location: Doncaster Racecourse
Notes: Lincoln Meeting
Contact Details: 01302 320066

April	
March or April, depending on tide	Oxford *v* Cambridge Boat Race *Location: Putney to Mortlake on the River Thames* *Notes: No tickets necessary* *Contact Details: 020 7379 3234 Press Office and* *sponsorship, London Tourist Board 0990 887711* *General information*

Grand National Steeplechase
Location: Aintree, Liverpool, Merseyside
Contact Details: 0151 522 2929

Berkeley Dress Show in aid of NSPCC
Location: Savoy Hotel, The Strand, London WC2

Notes: Debutantes modelling designer wear for charity
Contact Details: 020 7596 3724

The Craven Meeting at Newmarket
Location: Rowley Mile Course, Newmarket, Suffolk
Contact Details: 01638 663482

Chelsea Art Fair
Location: Chelsea Old Town Hall, Kings Road, London SW3
Contact Details: 01444 482514

Spring Meeting at Newbury
Location: Newbury Racecourse, Berkshire
Contact Details: 01635 40015

Whitbread Gold Cup
Location: Sandown Park Racecourse, Esher, Surrey
Contact Details: 01372 463072 General information, 01372 470047 Ticket hotline

The Flora London Marathon
Location: 26 miles from Blackheath to The Mall
Contact Details: 020 7620 4117

The Harrogate Spring Flower Show
Location: Great Yorkshire Showground, Harrogate, North Yorkshire
Notes: The largest in Europe
Contact Details: 01423 561049

The Royal Shakespeare Company Theatre Season Opens
Location: Stratford-on-Avon
Contact Details: 01789 295623 Box Office

The Royal Caledonian Ball
Location: Grosvenor House Hotel, Park Lane, London W1
Notes: Highland dress or White Tie for men, long dress for women. Dress code strictly enforced. Dinner or after dinner & breakfast tickets available
Contact Details: 020 8940 8079 the organiser's home phone number

May

The Guineas Meeting
Location: Rowley Mile Course, Newmarket, Suffolk
Notes: Booking advisable
Contact Details: 01638 663482 Box Office

Polo Season Starts

Chester Races
Location: The Roodee, Chester, Cheshire
Notes: Book early (by Jan advisable).

Excellent packages available
Contact Details: 01244 323170 Box Office

Dante Meeting
Location: York Racecourse, York
Notes: Book early (by Jan advisable)
Contact Details: 01904 620911 Box Office

Newbury International Spring Festival
Location: Newbury and surrounding areas
Notes: Primarily classical music from top performers.
Advance booking essential
Contact Details: 01635 32421 General information,
01635 522733 Box Office from early Feb

International Social Service of the United Kingdom
(ISS) Spring Fair
Location: Kensington Town Hall, London W8
Notes: Diplomats worldwide selling artefacts from their
countries for charity
Contact Details: 020 7735 8941

Badminton Horse Trials
Location: Badminton, Gloucestershire
Notes: Book ahead and ask for details of passes etc.
Contact Details: 01454 218272 General information,
01454 218375 Box Office

Royal Windsor Horse Show
Location: Windsor Home Park, Berkshire
Notes: Advanced booking advised
Contact Details: 01753 860633

Chatsworth Horse Trials
Location: Chatsworth House, Bakewell, Derbyshire
Contact Details: 01246 565300

Marlborough Cup Race
Location: Barbury Castle Racecourse,
Marlborough, Wiltshire
Notes: Race run over timber fences and county fair
Contact Details: 01672 511700

Chelsea Flower Show
Location: The grounds of the Royal Hospital, Chelsea,
London SW3
Notes: First two days RHS members only. Advanced
bookings only
Contact Details: 020 7344 4343

May/June   Royal Bath & West of England Show
Location: Shepton Mallet, Somerset
Contact Details: 01749 822200

Windsor Horse Trials
Location: Windsor Great Park, Berkshire
Contact Details: 01203 698856 British Horse Trials
Association

From 2001	Scottish Carriage Driving Championships *Location: St. Forts, Newport-on-Tay, Fife, Scotland* *Notes: Replaced in 2000 by Scottish Singles* *Championship in Aug* *Contact Details: 01382 541587* Glyndebourne Season Starts *Location: Glyndebourne Festival Opera, P.O. Box 264,* *Glyndebourne, Lewes, East Sussex BN8 5UW* *Notes: Postal bookings from April* *Contact Details: 01273 813813 Box Office*
May/June	*The Sunday Times* Hay Festival *Location: Various venues in the town* *Notes: Book from April. Ten day festival with well* *known worldwide authors taking part* *Contact Details: 01497 821217* Hay Children's Festival of the Arts *Location: Hay-on-Wye Community Centre Arts,* *children's theatre* *Contact Details: 0113230 4661* Blair Atholl Highland Gathering *Location: Blair Castle, Perthshire, Scotland* *Contact Details: 01796 481355 Estate Office*
Late May/ early June	The Bath International Music Festival *Location: Bath, Avon* *Notes: Around 100 musical events inc. classical,* *contemp' and jazz. Advance bookings essential* *Contact Details: 01225 463362* *General information and Box Office* Summer Shakespeare Season Opens *Location: Open-air Theatre, Regent's Park* *Notes: From April call the Box Office* *Contact Details: 020 7935 5756* *Box Office on 020 7486 2431*
June	
	The Louis Vuitton Classic *Location: Hurlingham Club, Fulham, London SW6* *Notes: Black tie. Vintage cars. Club members or by* *invitation only* *Contact Details: 020 7399 4040* The Royal Academy Summer Exhibition *Location: Burlington House, Piccadilly, London W1* *Contact Details: 020 7439 7438* Aldeburgh Festival of Music and the Arts *Location: Aldeburgh, Suffolk* *Notes: Founded by Benjamin Britten. Advance booking* *essential* *Contact Details: 01728 453543 Box Office*

Holland Park Opera Season Starts
Location: Holland Park, London
Notes: Season ends mid-Aug
Contact Details: 020 7602 7856 Box Office

Hampton Court Palace Festival of Music and Opera
Location: Hampton Court, Surrey
Notes: Held in the courtyard. Top-class productions and star performers. Advance booking essential
Contact Details: 020 8233 5800 Box Office,
020 8233 5178 Hospitality

Timeform Charity Raceday
Location: York Racecourse, York
Contact Details: 01904 620911

The Lords *v* Commons Tug of War
Location: Abingdon Green, London SW1
Notes: In aid of Macmillan Cancer Relief.
Very few tickets for sale
Contact Details: 020 7887 8271

Eastbourne International Ladies Tennis Championship
Location: Devonshire Park Centre, Eastbourne,
East Sussex
Notes: Advance booking essential
Contact Details: 01323 412000 General information
and Box Office

The Eton *v* Harrow Cricket Match
Location: Lords Cricket Ground, St John's Wood Rd,
London NW8
Contact Details: 020 7432 1066 MCC Ticket Office

Royal Cornwall Show
Location: Royal Cornwall Showground, Wadebridge,
Cornwall
Contact Details: 01208 812183 General information

Goodwood Festival Of Speed
Location: Goodwood House, Goodwood Park, Chichester,
Sussex
Notes: Cars from the golden age. Advance booking
essential for Sunday
Contact Details: 01243 755000 or 755055

The Mulberry Classic Tennis Tournament
Location: Hurlingham Club, Fulham, London SW6
Notes: Pro-Am and Veterans, in aid of NSPCC
Contact Details: 020 7491 4323

South of England Show
Location: South of England Centre,
Ardingly, Sussex
Notes: Including South of England Hound Show
Contact Details: 01444 892700

East of England Show
Location: East of England Showground, Peterborough,
Cambridgeshire
Contact Details: 01733 234451

Three Counties Show
Location: The Showground, Malvern
Contact Details: 01684 584900

The Royal Highland Show
Location: The Royal Highland Centre, Ingliston,
Edinburgh, Scotland
Contact Details: 0131 335 6200

The Royal Norfolk Show
Location: Dereham Rd, New Costessy,
Norwich, Norfolk
Contact Details: 01603 748931

Olympia Fine Art & Antiques Summer Fair
Location: Olympia, London
Contact Details: 020 7373 8141 Box Office

Grosvenor House Art & Antiques Fair
Location: Grosvenor House Hotel, Park Lane,
London W1
Contact Details: 020 7399 8100

Stella Artois Tennis Tournament
Location: Queen's Club, London W14
Notes: Advance booking essential
Contact Details: 020 7344 4000 Box Office,
020 7413 1414 General information

Trooping The Colour
Location: Horse Guards Parade, London SW1
Notes: Marking the Queen's Birthday. Tickets allotted by
postal ballot in March
Contact Details: 020 7414 2353

Wimbledon Lawn Tennis Championships
Location: All England Lawn Tennis & Croquet Club,
London SW19
Notes: The LTA hold a ballot for tickets. Ring their
number for details. There is a public ballot by post.
Write to The Ticket Office, All England Lawn Tennis
and Croquet Club, PO Box 9, Wimbledon, London SW19
5AE. Enclose a stamped addressed envelope
Contact Details: 020 7381 7000 Lawn Tennis
Association general information, 020 8944 1066
(AELTCC) general information

Holker Garden Festival
Location: Holker Hall & Gardens,
Cark-in-Cartmel, Grange-over-Sands,
Cumbria
Contact Details: 01539 558838

113

	Bramham Horse Trials *Location: Bramham Park, Wetherby, West Yorkshire* *Contact Details: 01937 844265* *General information and Box Office*
May/June	Alfred Dunhill Queen's Cup Final *Location: Guards Polo Club, Smiths Lawn,* *Windsor Great Park, Berkshire* *Contact Details: 01784 434212*
June/July	The Warwickshire Cup Polo *Location: Cirencester Park Polo Club,* *Cirencester Park, Glos.* *Contact Details: 01285 653225*
	The Derby Meeting *Location: Epsom Racecourse, Surrey* *Notes: Advance booking essential* *Contact Details: 01372 464348* *General information, 01372 470047 Box Office*
	Royal Ascot *Location: Ascot Racecourse, Berkshire* *Notes: Advance booking essential. Note special* *protocols, see Appendix II* *Contact Details: 01344 876876*
June/July	Garsington Opera *Location: Garsington Manor, Oxford* *Notes: Advance booking essential* *Contact Details: 01865 361636 Box Office*
	Biggin Hill International Air Fair *Location: Biggin Hill, Westerham, Kent* *Notes: Advanced booking advised* *Contact Details: 01959 540959*
June/July	Ludlow Festival *Location: Ludlow, Shropshire* *Notes: Open-air Shakespeare at the castle, music,* *and literary festival. Advance booking essential* *Contact Details: 01584 872150 Box Office*

July

1st	Red & Sika Stag Season opens *Location: Scotland*
June/July	
	Henley Royal Regatta *Location: Henley-on-Thames, Oxfordshire* *Contact Details: 01491 572 153*
	Coral Eclipse Meeting *Location: Sandown Park, Esher, Surrey* *Contact Details: 01372 463072*

Game Conservancy Scottish Fair
Location: Scone Palace, Perth, Scotland
Contact Details: 01620 850577

The Royal Show
Location: National Agricultural Centre,
Stoneleigh Park, Warwickshire
Contact Details: 01203 696969

April to
Sep

Test Cricket
Location: Lord's Cricket Ground, London NW8
Contact Details: 020 7289 1611 MCC General
information

Grange Park Opera Festival
Location: The Grange, Northington, nr. Alresford,
Hants. SO24
Notes: Advance booking essential
Contact Details: 020 7246 7567 Box Office

The Henley Festival of Music and the Arts
Location: Henley Royal Regattta Enclosure Site,
Henley-on-Thames, Oxfordshire
Notes: Advance booking essential
Contact Details: 01491 843400 General information,
01491 843404 Box Office (opens March)

The Cheltenham International Festival of Music
Location: Cheltenham, Glos.
Notes: Advance booking essential
Contact Details: 01242 521621 Administration,
01242 227979 Box Office

The Buxton Festival
Location: Buxton, Derbyshire.
Notes: Advance booking essential
Contact Details: 01298 70395 General information,
01298 72190 Box Office from March

The RHS Hampton Court Palace International Flower
Show
Location: The grounds of Hampton Court Palace, East
Molesey, Surrey
Notes: First two days members only.
Advance booking essential
Contact Details: 020 7957 4000
RHS members 020 7344 9966

The Traxdata Royal International Horse Show
Location: All England Jumping Course, Hickstead,
West Sussex
Contact Details: 01273 834315

July Meeting at Newmarket
Location: Newmarket, Suffolk
Contact Details: 01638 663482

Drumlanrig Horse Driving Trials
Location: Drumlanrig, Dumfries, Scotland
Contact Details: 01347 878789

Cornbury Park Horse Trials
Location: Charlbury, Oxfordshire
Contact Details: 01608 811276 Estate Office

The BBC Promenade Concert Season Opens
Location: Royal Albert Hall, London SW7
Notes: Book ahead, especially for last night
Contact Details: 020 7589 8212 Box Office

The Great Yorkshire Show
Location: Great Yorkshire Showground,
Harrogate, North Yorkshire
Notes: Includes Hound Show
Contact Details: 01423 541000

The Royal Welsh Show
Location: Llanelwedd, Builth Wells, Powys, Wales
Contact Details: 01982 553683

Formula One British Grand Prix
Location: Silverstone, Northants.
Notes: Advance booking essential
Contact Details: 01327 857271 General information,
01327 857273 Box Office

Final of the Gold Cup British Open Polo Championship
Location: Cowdray Park, Midhurst, Sussex
Contact Details: 01730 813257

The Royal Tournament. The last one was held in
1999. It will be replaced by the Royal Military Tattoo
in 2000 only

Peterborough Hound Show
Location: East of England Showground, Peterboro'
Contact Details: 01733 234451

De Beers Diamond Day at Ascot
Location: Ascot Racecourse, Berkshire
Contact Details: 01344 876876

Cartier International Polo
Location: Guards Polo Club, Smith's Lawn, Windsor
Great Park, Egham, Surrey TW20 0HP
Contact Details: 01784 434212 General information,
01784 437797 Box Office
(opens after Easter)

In 2000 only:
Aug

Glorious Goodwood
Location: Goodwood Racecourse, Chichester, Sussex
Notes: Annual members and guests only in the Richmond
Enclosure
Contact Details: 01243 755022

24th-30th	The Farnborough Air Show *Location: Farn'boro Aerodrome, Hants.* *Notes: Information from the Society of British Aerospace Companies* *Contact Details: 020 7227 1043* The Country Landowners Association Game Fair *Locations vary* *Contact Details: 01733 777344 Box Office*

August

1st	Red & Sika Stag and Fallow Buck Season Opens *Location: England & Wales*
1st	Fallow Buck Season Opens *Location: Scotland* Scandia Life Cowes Week *Location: Cowes, Isle of Wight* *Contact Details: 01983 293303 or Cowes Combined Clubs, 18 Bath Road, Cowes, IOW 01983 295744* Doubleprint British Open Horse Trials Championship *Location: Gatcombe Park, Glos.* *Contact Details: 01937 541811 Box Office* Honiton Agricultural Show and West of England Hound Show *Location: Devon* *Contact Details: 01404 891763* The Almeida at Malvern *Location: Malvern Theatre, Grange Road, Malvern, Worcs. WR14 3HB* *Notes: Renewed festival of theatre, originally established by George Bernard Shaw, with new productions from the cutting edge Islington theatre. Advance booking essential* *Contact Details: 01684 892277* Edinburgh International Festival *Location: Edinburgh, Scotland* *Notes: Advance booking essential* *Contact Details: 0131 473 2001* Edinburgh Military Tattoo *Location: The Esplanade, Edinburgh Castle, Scotland* *Contact Details: 0131 225 1188 Box Office and General information* Edinburgh Festival Fringe *Location: Edinburgh, Scotland* *Contact Details: 0131 226 5257 or 5259* The Glorious Twelfth Start of the grouse shooting season

Ballater Highland Games, Aberd'shire, Scotland
Contact Details: 01339 755771

Lowther Horse Driving Trials and Country Fair
Location: Lowther Castle, Penrith, Cumbria
In beautiful Lake District setting
Contact Details: 01931 712378

Scottish Championship Horse Trials
Location: Thirlestane Castle, Lauder, Berwickshire,
Scotland
Contact Details: 01896 860242 Box Office

Ebor Meeting
Location: York Racecourse, York
Contact Details: 01904 620911

August Meeting
Location: Goodwood Racecourse, Chichester, West
Sussex
Notes: Featuring the Tripleprint Celebration Mile
Contact Details: 01243 755022

Traxdata British Jumping Derby
Location: All England Jumping Course, Hickstead,
West Sussex
Notes: Replaces European Show Jumping Championships
Contact Details: 01273 834315

Epsom August Bank Holiday Meeting
Location: Epsom Racecourse, Epsom Downs, Surrey
Notes: Featuring the Moët & Chandon Silver Magnum
Contact Details: 01372 726311 General information

September

1st

Start of Partridge shooting season
Location: England, Scotland and Wales

Burghley Pedigree Chum Horse Trials
Location: Stamford, Lincolnshire
Contact Details: 01780 752131
General information and Box Office

Windsor Horse Driving Trials
Location: Windsor Great Park, Berkshire
Contact Details: 01347 878789

The National Trust Autumn Plant Sale
Location: Calke Abbey, Ticknall, Derbyshire
Contact Details: 01159 830278

Braemar Highland Gathering
Location: Braemar, Aberdeenshire, Scotland
Contact Details: 01339 755 377

	Chatsworth Country Fair *Location: Chatsworth House, Bakewell, Derbyshire* *Contact Details: 01263 711736*
	St Leger Festival Meeting *Location: Doncaster Racecourse, Doncaster, Yorkshire* *Notes: The flat racing season's oldest and final classic* *race* *Contact Details: 01302 320066*
	Blenheim International Horse Trials *Location: Woodstock, Oxfordshire* *Contact Details: 01993 813335*
	The Last Night of The Proms *Location: Royal Albert Hall, London SW7* *Notes: Advance booking essential, preferably by post* *Contact Details: 020 7589 8212*
	Chelsea Antiques Fair *Location: Chelsea Old Town Hall, Kings Rd, London SW3* *Contact Details: 01444 482514*
	Ayr Western Meeting Festival *Location: Ayr Racecourse, Ayrshire, Scotland* *Contact Details: 01292 264179*
End April- Sep	Perth Races *Location: Scone Palace, Perth, Scotland* *Contact Details: 01738 551597*
	Goodwood Revival Meeting *Location: Goodwood Motor Circuit, Goodwood* *Chichester, West Sussex* *Notes: The historic circuit now reopened for a festival of* *motor racing for the sport's golden age* *Contact Details: 01243 755055 or 755000*
	Festival of British Horse Racing *Location: Ascot Racecourse, Berkshire* *Notes: Featuring the Queen Elizabeth II Stakes* *Contact Details: 01344 876876*
30th	Salmon and Trout Seasons Close

October

1st	Start of Pheasant Shooting Season *Location: England, Scotland and Wales*
	The Horse of The Year Show *Location: Wembley Arena, Wembley, Middlesex* *Contact Details: 01203 693088*
	The Prix de l'Arc de Triomphe *Location: Longchamp, Paris, France* *Notes: Massive influx of the British making this event* *very much part of 'The Season'*

Contact Details: 00 33 1 49102030 & Horse Racing
Abroad 01444 441661

October Meeting
Location: Newmarket, Suffolk
Notes: Featuring the Camb'shire & Middle Park Stakes
Contact Details: 01638 663482

Tattersalls Yearling Sales
Location: Park Paddocks, Newmarket, Suffolk
Notes: See the high rollers and their agents bidding for
young hopeful racehorses of the future
Contact Details: 01638 665931

The LAPADA Show
Location: The Royal College of Art, Kensington Gore,
London SW7
Notes: Antique dealers fair
Contact Details: 020 7823 2511

The Cheltenham Festival of Literature
Location: Cheltenham, Glos. At Town Hall and other
venues
Notes: Advance booking essential
Contact Details: 01242 227979 Box Office: 01242
521621

Houghton Meeting
Location: Newmarket, Suffolk
Notes: Featuring the Champion Stakes and the
Cesarewitch
Contact Details: 01638 663482

20th	Red & Sika Stag Season Closes Location: Scotland
	Red & Sika Hind, Fallow and Roe Doe Season Opens Location: Scotland
31st	Roe & Fallow Buck Season Closes Location: England & Wales

November

1st	Start of Fox Hunting Season
1st	Red & Sika Hind and Roe & Fallow Doe Season Opens Location: England & Wales
	London to Brighton Veteran Car Run Location: 7.30a.m. start at Hyde Park Corner, London Notes: Brighton by 10.30a.m. at average speed of 20mph Contact Details: 01753 681736
	November Handicap Meeting Location: Doncaster Racecourse, Yorkshire Notes: To end the flat racing season Contact Details: 01302 320066

The Lord Mayor's Show
Location: City of London, EC1
Contact Details: 01483 577123

Olympia Fine Art & Antiques Winter Fair
Location: Olympia, London W14
Contact Details: 020 7373 8141 Olympia Box Office

The St Andrew's Ball
Location: Banqueting House, Whitehall, London SW1
Contact Details: Harry Verney 01962 771352

Cheltenham Countryside Race Day & Murphy's
Gold Cup
Location: Cheltenham Racecourse,Cheltenham, Glos.
Notes: Advance booking advised for Countryside Raceday
Contact Details: 01242 226226

Hennessy Cognac Gold Cup
Location: Newbury Racecourse, Berkshire
Contact Details: 01635 40015

December

10th

Season Closes
England, Scotland and Wales

The Royal Smithfield Show
Location: Earl's Court, Warwick Road, London SW5
Notes: Biennial. Next one in 2000
Contact Details: 020 7370 8226

The Varsity Match
Location: Twick'ham Rugby Ground, Twick'ham,
Middlesex
Contact Details: 020 7357 1000 Sponsorship information

International Show Jumping Championships
Location: Olympia, London W14
Contact Details: 01753 847900 General information,
0870 905 0600 Box Office

The Feathers Ball
Location: Bagleys Studios, York Way, King's Cross,
London N1
Notes: A must for public school teenagers. Advance
booking essential
Contact Details: Feathers Club Association: 020 7723
9167

Various Carol Services for charities
Location: St Paul's Church, Knightsbridge, London SW1
Contact Details: 020 7235 3460

Various Carol Services for charities
Location: St Giles-in-the-Fields Church, London WC2
Contact Details: 020 7240 2532

Various Carol Services for charities
Location: St Bride's Church, Fleet Street, London EC4
Contact Details: 020 7353 1301

Various Carol Services for charities
Location: St Michael's Church, Chester Sq, London SW1
Contact Details: 020 7730 8889

Various Carol Services for charities
Location: St Luke's Church, Sydney Street, Chelsea,
London SW3
Contact Details: 020 7351 7365

Various Carol Services for charities
Location: St Marylebone Parish Church, London NW1
Contact Details: 020 7935 7315

Various Carol Services for charities
Location: The Guards Chapel, Wellington Barracks,
London SW1
Notes: Tickets and information available from the
charities
Contact Details: 020 7930 4466 ext. 3228 General
information

Boxing Day Meeting
Location: Kempton Park Racecourse
Notes: Featuring the King George VI Chase
Contact Details: 01372 470047

Appendix VIII

Further Reading

For information on specific dates see the following:

- *The London and UK Datebook* – Published by Mary Kaye Eyerman (Tel: 020 7584 8462) is updated and printed four times a year, specialises in charity events.

- *Harpers & Queen* – See Diary Dates in its April issue. It has an excellent black leather-bound diary with seasonal events listed and some helpful information.

- *Tatler* – The May issue has The Veuve Clicquot Guide as a supplement.

- *The Field* – Possesses an excellent monthly Country Diary of events and gives dates of field sports seasons in full.

- *Horse & Hound* magazine – This has a weekly listings and two special show numbers in early spring which list all horsy events.